TEACHING
Reading
TO English
Language
Learners

TEACHING
Reading
TO English
Language
Learners

A REFLECTIVE GUIDE

THOMAS S. C. FARRELL

CORWIN
PRESS
A SAGE Company

For information:

Corwin Press
A SAGE Company
2455 Teller Road
Thousand Oaks, California 91320
www.corwinpress.com

SAGE Ltd.
1 Oliver's Yard
55 City Road
London EC1Y 1SP
United Kingdom

SAGE India Pvt. Ltd.
B 1/I 1 Mohan Cooperative
   Industrial Area
Mathura Road, New Delhi 110 044
India

SAGE Asia-Pacific Pte. Ltd.
33 Pekin Street #02-01
Far East Square
Singapore 048763

Printed in the United States of America.

Library of Congress Cataloging-in-Publication Data

Farrell, Thomas S. C. (Thomas Sylvester Charles)
Teaching reading to English language learners : a reflective guide/Thomas S. C. Farrell.
    p. cm.
Includes bibliographical references and index.
ISBN 978-1-4129-5734-2 (cloth : acid-free paper)
ISBN 978-1-4129-5735-9 (pbk. : acid-free paper)
    1. Reading—Handbooks, manuals, etc. 2. English language—Study and teaching—Foreign speakers—Handbooks, manuals, etc. I. Title.

LB1050.F343 2009
428.0071--dc22   2008019163

This book is printed on acid-free paper.

08   09   10   11   12   10 9 8 7 6 5 4 3 2 1

Acquisitions Editor:	Dan Alpert
Editorial Assistant:	Tatiana Richards
Production Editor:	Libby Larson
Copy Editor:	Cate Huisman
Typesetter:	C&M Digitals (P) Ltd.
Proofreader:	Penelope Sippel
Indexer:	Rick Hurd
Cover Designer:	Rose Storey
Graphic Designer:	Lisa Riley

Contents

Preface

*T*eaching Reading to English Language Learners: A Reflective Guide is for
ELL reading teachers and any other teachers who teach English reading to students whose first language is not English, that is, students who
are learning English as a second or subsequent language as well as those
learning English as a foreign language. It will be helpful whether or not
these teachers have a background in teaching ELLs or ESL (English
as a second/subsequent language) learners or EFL (English as a foreign
language) learners. It encourages each teacher to develop his or her own
philosophy of teaching reading to ELLs, a philosophy that is based on
understanding the key principles of teaching reading to ELLs. The
approaches and methods that are outlined in each chapter should not be
taken as prescription; rather, the contents can and should be adapted in
many different ways for many different contexts as reading teachers make
decisions based on their students' individual needs.

Teaching Reading to English Language Learners: A Reflective Guide can be
used by individual teachers or by pairs and groups of teachers informally,
or it can be used as a textbook for preservice or inservice language teacher
development courses as well as for language teacher preparation courses in
MA/MEd programs. The book can also be used as a source book for heads
and principals of schools and institutions or by directors and administrators
of school districts who reflect themselves or want to encourage their language
teachers to reflect on the teaching of reading to ELLs.

STRUCTURE OF THE BOOK

Each chapter attempts to help teachers uncover aspects of their work that
specifically relate to teaching reading to English Language Learners.
Chapter 1, Teaching Reading to ELLs, outlines some principles of teaching
reading to ELLs. These principles lead to individual chapters that form
most of the contents of this book. Chapter 2, Reflecting on the Reading
Process, encourages the reading teacher to reflect on the reading process

for teacher-as-reader and as a teacher of reading to ELLs. Chapter 3, Teaching Reading Fluency and Comprehension to ELLs, discusses the concepts of reading fluency and comprehension and how to teach ELLs to increase both. Chapter 4, Teaching Reading Strategies to ELLs, outlines some of the activities that teachers can consider when teaching these strategies to their students. Chapter 5, Teaching Text Structure to ELLs, examines how to recognize different text types and their schematic structures, and it examines how parts of a text are joined together. Chapter 6, Teaching Vocabulary to ELLs, outlines how teachers can explicitly teach various strategies so that students can increase their word banks. Chapter 7, Planning Effective Reading Lessons for ELLs, covers various issues that teachers need to consider when planning effective reading lessons. Chapter 8, Promoting Extensive Reading for ELLs, outlines and discusses how teachers can promote extensive reading so their students will eventually read more texts on their own both for information and for pleasure. Chapter 9, Authentic Reading Assessment for ELLs, discusses various ways teachers can authentically assess their students' learning of reading.

Thus, once reading teachers come to understand the how and why of what they do in class and have done in previous reading classes, they can then take steps that will carry them along the path to making more informed decisions in the classroom about the teaching of reading to ELLs, because now they have more choices.

REFLECTIONS

Throughout the book you will see **Reflections** in different places in each chapter. These are designed to give you some time out to reflect on various aspects of teaching reading and can be completed alone or with another teacher. They can be used before, during, or after reading. You can also reproduce many of these **Reflections** to use with your students. Of course, the **Reflections** can and should be redesigned to take your students' needs into consideration. Alternatively, you can skip these until you have read the chapter, or indeed, if you are very busy (what teacher of reading is not!), you can skip them completely until you have time during your vacation.

Acknowledgments

I t would not have been possible to learn what I have included in this book without the help and guidance of many people I encountered along the way in various institutions in which I worked around the world but in particular those I met during my time teaching the Reading Module at the National Institute of Education, Singapore. My colleagues at that time enlightened me with respect to many of the activities outlined in this book, and I thank them so much for shaping much of what I know about reading and the reading process. Specifically I would like to thank Anthony Seow, Vanita Saravannan, and Lawrence Zhang for the insight they provided during the seven years I joined them as team members for the Reading Module.

As always this book would not have been possible without the support of my family: Mija, Sarah, and Ann. I also thank Corwin Press, and especially Dan Alpert, for giving me this opportunity to share my ideas with you, the reader.

Corwin Press gratefully acknowledges the contributions of the following reviewers:

James Becker, Teacher/Administrator
Toronto, Ontario, Canada

Deb Bible, Literacy Teacher and Coach
CUSD 300, West Dundee, IL

Amie Brown, Eighth Grade English Language Arts Lead Teacher
Ashworth Middle School, Calhoun, GA

Lucia deSombre Malo, Former Instructor
Utah Valley State College, Logan, UT

Rick Froehbrodt, English Language Development Teacher
King Elementary School, El Cajon, CA

Norma Godina-Silva, Director of ELL Services
Edison Schools, El Paso, TX

Gladys González, ELL Teacher
Whittier Elementary School, Boise, ID

Angie Koppang, Associate Professor of Educational Administration
University of South Dakota, Vermillion, SD

About the Author

 **Thomas S. C. Farrell** is a professor in applied linguistics at Brock University, Canada. He has been involved with ESL and applied linguistics for the past 27 years and has written extensively on topics such as reflective practice, language teacher development, and language teacher education. His recent books include *Reflective Practice in Action* (2004, Corwin Press), *Reflecting on Classroom Communication in Asia* (2004), *Professional Development for Language Teachers* (2005, coauthored with Jack Richards), and *Succeeding With English Language Learners: A Guide for Beginning Teachers* (2006, Corwin Press).

1

Teaching Reading to ELLs

Reading can be one of the greatest pleasures we experience throughout our lives. Reading helps us in many ways: It entertains, educates, communicates, and informs us about the past, the present, and even the future. Many (but not all) children learn how to read in their first language before they enter the school system, and once in school, all depend on their teachers to help further develop their reading skills so that eventually they can discover the joy of reading. In many of our classrooms today, we find that many of our students do not use English as their first language and that many English language learners (ELLs— I use the term *English language learner* throughout this book to refer to students who are learning English as a second or subsequent language as well as those learning English as a foreign language) learning to read use similar, but not the same, processes as beginning readers learning to read in their first language. For example, many times, beginning ELLs plunge into a text when they start to read, but when they meet a difficult word or confusing sentence or paragraph, their reading grinds to a halt and becomes painful, boring, no fun, or too difficult for them to continue, and so some give up trying to learn how to read in the second/subsequent language.

Some of the problems associated with ELLs struggling to read can unfortunately be attributed to particular methods of reading instruction that either test rather than teach reading or that do not take into consideration the differences between learning to read in a first and a second/ subsequent language. For instance, when a reading teacher asks his or her students to read a passage and answer the comprehension questions that follow (or the *ten-question syndrome*, as my former colleagues at the National Institute of Education in Singapore called it), or to write a summary, or to explain the meaning of individual words and then to write the words in a sentence, all these are *testing* and not really teaching reading. Testing reading has a place in the curriculum but only after we teach our students *how* to read. We must also recognize that students learning to read in their first language have more knowledge of grammar and vocabulary than ELLs learning to read in a second/subsequent language. Furthermore, ELLs also have varying levels of English language proficiency that have an impact on reading comprehension.

The good news is that we *can teach* reading to our ELLs. Throughout this book I propose that the goal of teaching reading to ELLs is for our students to be able to turn "learning to read" into "reading to learn" (Carrell, 1998) so that they can become fully functioning members of our society. This chapter first discusses some of the differences between learning to read in a first language and learning to read in a subsequent language, because we cannot assume that second language readers from different language backgrounds (e.g., Chinese, Hmong, Spanish) will carry out the reading processes in the same ways when they learn to read in English. Then it outlines some principles of teaching reading to ELLs that lead to individual chapters, which form most of the contents of this book.

In addition, because this is a book about teaching reading, and because many of the activities in the book involve prereading and postreading activities, I also include such activities (under the heading Reflection) for readers to use when reading the contents of this book. I use one term for these activities: *reflection*, and this includes reflection-for-reading (or prereading reflection), reflecting-during-reading (or during-reading reflection), and reflection-on-reading (or postreading reflection). Thus I hope you can see that I am attempting to practice what I am preaching.

REFLECTION

- What do you think are the main differences between learning to read in a first language and a second/subsequent language?

LEARNING TO READ IN A FIRST AND A SECOND/SUBSEQUENT LANGUAGE

Most of the research that has been conducted on reading has focused on students learning to read in their first language, but an increasing amount of recent reading research has related to students learning to read in their second and subsequent languages. However, many of these studies have been based on the original first language studies, and as Grabe and Stoller (2002, p. 40) have noted, "One of the most difficult talks we face as reading teachers is deciding how to make use of reading research for our own purposes [as teachers of ELLs]." That said, there is general agreement that ELLs begin reading in the second/subsequent language with a different knowledge base (e.g., more world knowledge, more developed cognitive abilities) than they had when they started to read in their first language (Grabe, 1991), and this has an impact on how we teachers should approach reading instruction.

The ways in which second language comprehension processes and instruction may differ from first language contexts can be classified as follows (adapted from Aebersold & Field, 1997, and Grabe & Stoller, 2002):

- Linguistic differences between the first and the second/subsequent language.
- Individual differences between first and second/subsequent language readers.
- Sociocultural differences between the first and second/subsequent language.

LINGUISTIC DIFFERENCES

Research has suggested that there are differing amounts of lexical, grammatical, and discourse knowledge at the initial stages of first and second language reading. For example, Grabe and Stoller (2002) point out that by the age of six, most first language readers are "ready" to read because they have already learned (tacitly) grammatical structures of their first language, and they already have nearly 7,000 words stored in their heads. However, ELLs do not have this word bank to draw on when learning to read in the second/subsequent language. Thus, having them sound out a word to "discover" its meaning, a popular reading activity in many reading classes the world over, is not very effective, although it may still be effective for first language students.

In addition, because ELL readers do not have a tacit knowledge of the second language grammar, they need some additional instruction in building a foundation of structural knowledge and text organization for more effective reading comprehension (see Chapter 5, Teaching Text Structure to ELLs). Teachers of ELLs will probably need to teach vocabulary and discourse structure to their students from the very beginning of their reading classes, because most ELL readers will not have been exposed to many English language texts (through reading that is). So they will not have been able to build up any real processing skills nor the large recognition vocabulary that readers learning in their first language have. In fact, first language readers already have spent years building up this amount of exposure to print needed to develop fluency and automaticity in reading.

Another aspect of linguistic differences between two languages that teachers of ELLs may want to consider, because it may influence second language reading comprehension, concerns the differences between the ELLs' first language and the second/subsequent language they are learning to read in, in this case English. Grabe and Stoller (2002, p. 47), for example, have pointed out that ELL students whose first language is a Romance language (e.g., Spanish, French, Italian, and Portuguese) tend to focus greater amounts of attention on "the ends of the words because there is more grammatical information there than in English," while readers whose first language is Chinese, Japanese, or Korean "will make greater use of visual processing" than readers of English, because of their "first language orthography." These linguistic differences can lead to variations in reading rates and reading fluency, and thus teachers of reading to ELLs may want to become more aware of their students' first language orthography and rhetorical structures. This can be accomplished by surveying the students about these on the very first day of instruction.

REFLECTION

- Why would it be important to become more aware of your ELLs' educational and linguistic backgrounds?
- I suggested above that you could survey your ELLs on the first day about their educational and linguistics backgrounds. How would you go about this? What questions would you ask them and why?
- What would be the implications for you as a teacher of reading to ELLs if you discovered that a student was illiterate in his or her first language? How would this impact your teaching of reading?
- What would be the implications for you as a teacher of reading to ELLs if you discovered that a student's first language writing system was very similar to English or very different from that of English?
- What would be the implications for you as a teacher of reading to ELLs if you discovered that a student could or could not describe and discuss rules of his or her own first language?
- Which students in the previous two questions do you think would improve faster as readers of English and why?

INDIVIDUAL DIFFERENCES

Just as linguistic differences between the first and second/subsequent language influence the rate and success of learning to read, proficiency levels in the first language can also influence reading abilities and successes for ELLs. Research suggests that ELLs who are more literate in their first language are more able to transfer reading skills from their first language, although the exact way ELL readers can positively transfer this knowledge is still not clear. Koda (2005) suggests that ELLs who are less literate in their first language cannot really be expected to transfer many supporting resources to their second/subsequent language reading contexts.

In addition, individual ELLs tend to differ in terms of their *cognitive development* and *learning style*, especially when they start to study in the second language (Aebersold & Field, 1997). For example, the reading strategies of a six-year-old learning to read in a second/subsequent language are quite different from those of a 20-year-old learning to read in the second/subsequent language in terms of world knowledge and reading strategies acquired in the first language. So teachers of reading to ELLs may have to consider different approaches for children than for adults.

REFLECTION

- How would different levels of language proficiency impact your teaching of reading to ELLs?
- How would you approach teaching of reading to young ELLs and adult ELLs? Would it be the same or different?
- Rivera (1999) has suggested that ELLs may benefit from using their native language literacy skills, because they can transfer some basic skills in reading from their first to their second/subsequent language. Do you agree, and if so, what skills could they transfer? If you disagree, why do you think such skills are not transferable?

SOCIOCULTURAL DIFFERENCES

In some cultures literacy in the form of written texts may not be as common as it is in English. So teachers may want to consider what it means to be literate and how literacy is valued, used, and displayed in their ELL students' first languages. In addition, texts are not always organized in the same linear display in other languages as they are in English. For example, although this is controversial, Kaplan (1987) has pointed out that the linear approach to English language includes a writer responsibility to make the text clear and direct to readers, and this is in direct contrast to the spiral structure and indirectness of many Asian languages, which have a tradition of reader responsibility to extract meaning from the text.

More specifically, there can be cultural differences in the ways texts express interpersonal relations with the reader in terms of presence or absence of personal pronouns and in terms of whether it is the writer's responsibility to provide details or the reader's responsibility to read between the lines. So, teachers may want to become more aware of their ELL students' attitudes toward different types of text, their purposes for reading, and the types of reading skills and strategies they use in their first language. Teachers may also be interested in understanding their students' use of different reading skills and strategies in the second/subsequent language, their beliefs about the reading process (e.g., the use of inference, memorization, nature of comprehension), their knowledge of text types in their first language (their formal schemata), and their background knowledge (their content schemata). This is because *all* of the above influence the level of success their ELLs will achieve while learning to read.

REFLECTION

- Read the following short paragraph (from Eskey, 2002, p. 6) and answer the 10 questions that follow.

  It was the day of the big party. Mary wondered if Johnny would like a kite. She ran to her bedroom, picked up her piggy bank, and shook it. There was no sound.

  1. Does this story take place in the past, present, or future?
  2. What did Mary wonder?
  3. What does the word *wonder* signal?
  4. What is a *kite?*
  5. What is a *piggy bank?*
  6. What kind of party do you think this is?
  7. Are Mary and Johnny adults or children?
  8. How is the kite related to the party?
  9. Why did Mary shake her piggy bank?
  10. Mary has a big problem; what is it?

- What do you notice about the reading skills and strategies you used to answer questions 1 to 5 and questions 6 to 10?

- Did you use the same or different skills and strategies to answer both sets of questions? Explain.

I usually answer questions like 1 to 5 by only decoding the text, because all the relevant information is included in the text. However, in order to answer questions 6 to 10, I must have certain knowledge of Western culture and particularly of birthday parties. This knowledge is not directly in the text, and some ELLs may not possess it. In order to make meaning from the text in the previous **Reflection** activity, ELLs must engage in what Eskey (2002, p. 6) has called "parallel processing," whereby the reader simultaneously decodes and engages in cultural interpretations of the text. This invisible process of reading produces enormous challenges for teachers of ELLs, because reading does not "generate any product that a teacher can see or hear or respond to" (Eskey, 2002, p. 6).

From the discussion above, I present the following principles of teaching reading; much of the following chapters are based on these principles.

PRINCIPLES OF TEACHING READING TO ELLs

The previous section outlined various differences (backed by research) between learning to read in a first language and in a second/subsequent language. Of course, we may wish that methods of teaching reading, either for first or subsequent language, had caught up with the results of these various research studies, but unfortunately this is not the case. In fact, there is still a general lack of agreement as to how reading should be taught to children in their first language. As Glasgow and Farrell (2007) have pointed out, in the United States the debates over the best teaching methods have even extended from educational into political and religious circles.

Thankfully though, the International Reading Association (IRA) has recently recognized that there is "no single method or single combination of methods that can successfully teach all children to read." It is best if teachers have a knowledge of multiple methods for teaching reading and are also aware of the learning styles and preferences of the children in their care, so they can "create the appropriate balance of methods needed for the children they teach" (International Reading Association, 2006). The IRA also suggests that "professionals who are closest to the children must be the ones to make the decisions about what reading methods to use," that is, that individual teachers should make this decision (IRA, 2006). In addition, August and Shanahan (2006) have recently noted that regardless of the type of program offered by a school (bilingual, dual immersion, sheltered instruction, or ESL), the keys to success are that the program is based on a solid understanding of the research and that it is staffed by qualified educators.

This book suggests too that teachers of reading to ELLs not only utilize the research and methods outlined here but, more crucially, adapt them to their own students' needs and to the individual contexts they are teaching in. With this in mind, I now present eight principles of reading instruction for ELLs that can be adapted to each particular reading teacher's context. These principles are derived from both the research in learning to read in a first language (the dominant research that exists for second/subsequent language reading specialists and that forms the basis for much of the second/subsequent language reading research) and the existing research in learning to read in a second/subsequent language. Each principle forms a chapter in the proceeding pages of this book.

1. Reflect on reading.

A good starting principle for teachers of ELLs would be to reflect on their own reading behaviors, the nature of reading, and the reading process itself. Just because we are fluent readers does not mean that we can explain how we read, why we read what we read (the methods we employ), or that we actually understand the reading process. We need to examine the reading process in order to develop a philosophy of teaching reading, and we should also examine our own reading habits and behaviors to make sure they are not too far removed from what we ask our students to do.

After reflecting on our own reading behaviors and the reading process itself, we can now begin to reflect on how we currently teach reading in our classes. We can do this by asking another teacher to observe us as we teach or by using a video or audio recorder to become more aware of what we actually do. The main point of this first principle is that teachers of ELLs should look at themselves as readers and at their understanding of the reading process first, before they examine what is happening in their reading classes, so that they can make more informed decisions about how they want to teach reading to ELLs.

2. Teach fluency and comprehension.

Related to the first principle of reflecting on our practice of reading, we will now want to focus on the teaching of reading, both comprehension and fluency. Most first language learners read for general comprehension purposes that include getting some information from the text or just reading for pleasure. This type of reading for general comprehension requires an ability to understand information in a text and also an ability to interpret it appropriately. In order to achieve this comprehension, most first language readers tend to read at rates between 200 and 300 words per minute, and so we can see how reading fluency is closely connected to reading comprehension. Fluent readers probably need to know about 95 percent or more of the words they see in texts, and ELLs may not know this percentage of the words they read. So teachers of ELLs may have to focus their instruction not only on reading strategies but also on how to make use of discourse information (text structure) to build both comprehension and fluency.

3. Teach reading strategies.

We can distinguish between skills of reading and strategies for reading. Skills of reading, according to Grabe and Stoller (2002, p. 15), include "linguistic processing abilities that are relatively automatic in their use and combinations," such as word recognition. Strategies are "a set of abilities that readers have conscious control over but are also relatively automatic such as skipping a word we may not know when reading" (Grabe & Stoller, 2002, p. 15). Reading strategies indicate how readers make sense of what they read and what they do when they do not understand a passage. Research suggests that effective reading strategies can be taught to ELLs and that our students can benefit from such instruction. Strategy instruction also develops student knowledge about the reading process, introduces ELLs to specific strategies; and provides them with opportunities to discuss and practice strategies while reading. That said, the ultimate goal of reading instruction is not to teach individual reading strategies but rather to develop strategic readers.

4. Teach text structures.

Research in first language reading has suggested that students who can recognize and follow a text's basic discourse organization can also later recall more information from that text. In addition, students who have knowledge of discourse organization, so that they used the organization to later recall information from texts, are also better readers. Making ELLs aware of how texts are organized also helps them with their reading fluency, comprehension, and efficiency. Consequently, it seems plausible that we specifically teach ELLs how different texts are structured and organized and even how paragraphs are organized and cohesive.

5. Teach vocabulary building.

A large vocabulary is essential for ELLs, not only for reading purposes but also for all other related language skills such as speaking and writing. In fact, for ELLs, as Eskey and Grabe (1988, p. 232) have suggested, "Words seem to have a status in language akin to that of molecules in physical structures, and good readers become remarkably adept at recognizing thousands of them at a glance." It seems logical then if we have ELL students read a lot, then they will be exposed to many new words and will learn and retain a lot of these new words. In fact, research in first language reading suggests readers will learn one to three new words out of every 20 new words that they are exposed to while reading through such incidental learning. However, for ELLs we need to also explicitly teach vocabulary by instructing students to guess word meanings from the context in order to understand unfamiliar vocabulary they may encounter while reading. They will also need to improve their vocabulary identification skills by doing rapid word-recognition exercises.

6. Promote extensive reading.

If I were to say the word *textbook* to you, what is the first thing that pops into your mind? Is it pain or is it pleasure? Do you have a happy feeling? Many would still sigh and say they already feel bored with that word, because most of the textbooks they used at school were boring. So, why do we continue to produce the same boring textbooks for our students to read? When we ask our students to take out their textbooks, they usually equate this with pain—they find these books very dull and uninteresting. Now, however, we reading teachers can provide some opportunities for our students to use alternative reading materials by promoting extensive reading of materials *they* are interested in.

7. Plan effective reading classes.

Teachers of ELLs also need to consider how to plan reading lessons that are effective so that they can help move their students from a position of *learning to read* to *reading to learn* as mentioned above. Planning for language lessons may be different from planning for other content lessons, because the same concepts may need to be reinforced time and again using different methods, especially for beginning and intermediate students. Richards (1990, pp. 89–90) suggests that an effective reading teacher should "develop (and convey these to his or her students) specific instructional objectives for his class that reflect the teaching of reading at all levels of proficiency." Some of these objectives include

- having students develop an awareness of reading strategies necessary for successful reading comprehension,
- having them expand vocabulary and techniques to increase their vocabulary bank,

- having them develop an awareness of linguistic and rhetorical structures found in different reading texts,
- increasing their reading speed and fluency, and
- providing practice in extensive reading skills.

8. Use authentic reading assessment.

When we think of a test, we see students sitting down with pencil or pen and writing on a piece of paper at a particular time in a particular place. They could be answering questions on a midterm exam, a final exam, a quiz, or an end-of-chapter test. Here, a teacher is trying to find out what the students have learned as a result of taking a specific course. These are called traditional paper-and-pencil tests, and more often than not they focus only on students' memorization abilities and not on what students can do with the information.

However, the word *assessment* is more encompassing in that it means more of an ongoing process that includes tests and also other kinds of measurement not possible with paper-and-pencil tests. In other words, to assess a student authentically does not always mean to test the student. Thus, assessment, as the word is used in this book, includes both the traditional, quantitative, paper-and-pencil tests and also such qualitative items as portfolio assessment, peer assessment, self-reports, anecdotal records, and attitude scales.

REFLECTION

- What do you think of each of the eight principles outlined above?
- Can you add more of your own principles for teaching reading to ELLs?

CONCLUSION

This chapter has noted several differences between learning to read in a first and a second/subsequent language. Although the research on teaching reading as a second/subsequent language has not yet caught up with the vast amount of research that has been conducted in learning to read in a first language, this chapter outlined eight principles of reading instruction that are based on a combination of the results of this research; each of these principles will be discussed in more detail in the chapters that follow.

2 Reflecting on the Reading Process

This chapter is about teachers reflecting on the act of reading and the reading process itself. It is important for reading teachers to examine the nature of reading and the reading process, because as Tierney and Pearson (1994) have suggested, "If teachers understand the nature of reading comprehension and learning from a text, they will have the basis for evaluating and improving learning environments" (p. 496) for their students learning to read. Of course, all teachers of reading know how to read themselves (otherwise they would not be teachers); however, if you ask any teacher of reading to explain the actual reading process (how it happens), he or she may have a difficult time explaining exactly what happens when a reader comprehends a reading passage. Teachers of reading who have tried to explain the reading process to children, parents, or even other teachers realize just how complicated it is, and one reason for this is that the comprehension process happens inside our heads and so remains hidden from us. Thus, this chapter helps you, the reading teacher, to reflect on the reading process for you as a reader and as a teacher of reading to ELLs.

REFLECTION

- What is reading?
- How do you read? Explain the process.
- What is the first thing you do when you read an article or a book?

- What do you do when you read? Do you underline important text, highlight important text, do something else, or do nothing else?
- What do you do if you encounter a word you do not understand while reading?
- What do you do if you encounter a whole paragraph you do not understand while reading?
- What do you do to remember important information while reading?

WHAT IS READING?

If you ask most fluent readers to explain how they read, they may have a difficult time explaining it in detail. Try to answer the questions posed above, and especially try to explain how you read (the process). It is not easy to explain, because no two readers read in the same way. It is important, however, for reading teachers to become aware of the reading process in order to be able to anticipate "the types of processes and potential problems" (Aebersold & Field, 1997, p. 19) their students may experience when reading. Reading is a complex process, because it involves both conscious and subconscious actions by the reader. The actions that occur subconsciously cannot be seen by anyone. Eskey (2002, p. 5) suggests that reading is a process of obtaining information from a written text that does not involve "converting written language into spoken language." This poses our first problem for teachers of reading to ELLs, because reading aloud (which is always speaking) is a favorite classroom activity in their reading classes.

REFLECTION

- Is reading aloud real reading?

The question posed above has caused some controversy over the years in both first language and second/subsequent language reading classes. The issue of reading aloud with both first language students and ELLs is that it can degenerate into an exercise of pronunciation or reading with expression in which the reader does not necessarily understand what he or she is reading (Eskey, 2002). In addition, when reading aloud is used frequently, it can actually slow down reading speed, and this may not be useful for ELLs. However, because we cannot "see" reading, reading aloud may be the only way we can "hear" and "see" how our ELLs read (check how they decode a written text). As such, we can use the activity sometimes, especially if we organize the activity efficiently by stopping readers periodically to ask them to rephrase what they have just read or to predict what will follow in the text, or to ask other students in the class similar questions to make sure all are following. In addition, research by Amer (1997) has indicated that when teachers read aloud in class, this may have a significant positive effect on ELLs' reading comprehension. So, merely sounding out the words (reading aloud) is not real reading, because we also need to understand what we are reading in that text.

REFLECTION

- *Quickly* look at Figure 2.1; read it (take only a few seconds); then hide the figure and write down (do not copy) what you see.

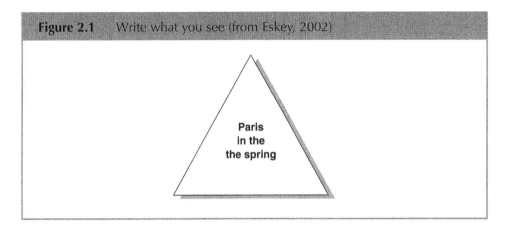

Figure 2.1   Write what you see (from Eskey, 2002)

**Paris
in the
the spring**

What did you write for the reflective activity? Did you notice the repeated word *the* ("the the") after "in"? What is written is "Paris in *the the* spring"; however, what most fluent readers see when they read quickly is "Paris in the spring" (only one *the*), because this makes the most sense to them as they read. In other words, they read for meaning, and they do not consciously process the meaning of each and every word.

As Eskey (2002) notes, the fact that fluent readers fail to see the second *the* makes them "good" readers. Struggling readers tend to be able to repeat *all* of the words they read but may not understand what the words mean. When fluent readers read, their eyes take in a chunk at a time, and that is why they come up with meaning. Their eyes move in "jerky movements called saccades" (Eskey, 2002, p. 5). Try this activity with your own students.

Good readers, then, do not have to see everything in a text to be able to decode its meaning. Of course, reading is more than trying to decode words in a text, because we must also be able to understand what all these words mean when taken together as a whole.

REFLECTION

- Read the following short paragraph (from Mikulecky, 1990), and write down what you think the paragraph is about.

  A newspaper is better than a magazine. The seashore is a better place than the street. At first it is better to run than to walk. You may have to try several times. It takes some skill, but it's easy to learn. Even young children can enjoy it. Once successful, complications are minimal. Birds seldom get too close. Rain, however, soaks in very fast. Too many people doing the same thing can also cause problems. One needs a lot of room. If there are no complications, it can be very peaceful. A rock will serve as an anchor. If things break loose, however, you will not get a second chance.

What did you write down for the meaning of the paragraph above? The "answer" is flying a kite, but no doubt many skilled readers could also make a case for some different topics. This is, in fact, a text that is easy to decode but difficult to comprehend. The main point here is that simply decoding the text will not be sufficient to make the overall meaning of the paragraph clear, because readers must also engage in active interpretation of the text by linking the paragraph to their prior knowledge of the world. We can add to our definition of reading, then, that the text we are reading may trigger something in our brain that is full of knowledge (schema) and that relates any new information we get from the text to what we already know. In other words, we construct and assign our own meaning to the text we are reading, or as Smith (1978) acknowledges, "What the brain tells the eye is more important than what the eye tells the brain" (p. 96).

REFLECTION

- Try to re-create the following short story by quickly filling in the blanks with what you think is the correct word. (I thank my colleagues at the National Institute of Education, Singapore, for showing me this type of reading activity.) As you fill in the various blanks, try to monitor what you do when you read.

Once _____ _____ _____, there was _____ _____ prince named _____. He lived in a big _____. Although Charles _____ _____ _____ _____ castle, he _____ _____ happy. He was very _____ because he had no _____. Day _____ _____ he would look out the _____, hoping to _____. One _____ his fairy _____ asked him _____ he _____ like _____ _____ _____ _____. Of _____ _____ _____ _____ yes. They played _____ _____ _____.

When you filled in the blanks for the activity above, what did you notice about your own reading behaviors? Did you depend on the text itself completely for meaning, or did you use some other information? If you utilized other information, where did you get this from? For example, did you know the name of the handsome prince was Charles before you saw it, or did you give the prince a different name? Did you realize this was the fairy story style with the beginning as *Once upon a time* and the end as, *they played happily ever after?* Did you put these in without thinking, or did you start and end the story a completely different way? If so, what does this tell you about your reading process?

There are many questions that can be asked about this short passage reconstruction, but the main point is that it gives you as a reader (and teacher of reading) an opportunity to reflect on your own reading. All these reflective activities suggest, as Johnson (1983) has observed, that each reader builds a model of personal meaning that "the writer is *assumed* [italics added] to have intended" (p. 17). So, on one side we have the writer's intentions (but we cannot talk to the writer about these), and on the other we have the reader's perceptions of what was written, and of course, the writer's intentions do not always align with the reader's understanding. That said, we can say that the reader is *actively* interacting with the text in order to create meaning of some sort; it just does not happen by itself. In addition, as the fairy story reflection shows, in order for ELLs to be able to interpret a text, they must have the cultural knowledge associated with the text (in this case, with fairy stories or the fairy story schema) in order to be able to comprehend it.

REFLECTION

- Reading Kills
  - What is the first thing that comes into your head when you read this heading and why?

MODELS OF READING

Different readers will have different reactions to the heading ("Reading Kills") in the above reflective activity. Some will read the exact words and think that something about reading has killed someone or something of the like, but what if I included the second part of the same subheading as follows? "Reading Kills: It Kills Ignorance!" The main idea of the heading of course is that if one can read, then one will not be ignorant. In other words, we use different processes when we read.

Different researchers have different opinions of what processes are involved when we read, and these have been presented and discussed mostly in terms of particular models of reading. One model of reading, called the *top-down processing model*, argues that reading is directed by the brain (associated with schema theory) that readers bring their prior knowledge and experiences to the text as they read, and that this influences how they understand and interpret a text. In fact the extreme version of this model suggests that readers will only continue to read a text as long as it confirms their prior expectations. This top-down reading process can be explained as follows: After first looking at a passage or a text, readers guess or predict what it will be about based on their prior knowledge and experience of the topic. They can do this after reading the title, the headings, and the subheadings and glancing quickly through the text. They then continue to read the text seeking confirmation of their understanding of the topic. So readers using a top-down approach will try to fit the text into the knowledge and experiences they already have.

A second model is called the *bottom-up processing model*. It suggests that a reader takes meaning from the text itself, from each word and sentence and from how the text is organized, in order to construct meaning from that text only; this model is thus associated with phonics. In this approach, information is first processed in the smallest sound units and then moves to letters, words, phrases, and full sentences. Understanding or comprehension of the text will ultimately depend on the reader's knowledge of vocabulary and syntax. The bottom-up process can be explained as follows: When we read, one thing we do is extract the propositions from the text. How? By breaking sentences into their constituent parts and constructing the propositions from there. Comprehension then depends on the propositions we have extracted, which serve as the basis of what we understand and recall (J. C. Richards, personal communication). This can be seen as the opposite of the top-down approach; instead of working from meaning to text (top-down), this model has a reader working from text to meaning (with a focus at word and sentence level).

Yet another model of how reading works with ELLs is called the *interactive processing model* (Stanovich, 1980) and argues that both approaches explained above, the top-down and bottom-up processes, occur simultaneously when a person reads a text. (We use the brain *and* the text for meaning making.) This is sometimes related to the Balanced Approach in first language reading research, because it provides us with a more balanced view of the important contributions of both the text we are reading and our own creation of meaning from our background knowledge and experiences. Figure 2.2 outlines how this interactive process may work for fluent readers.

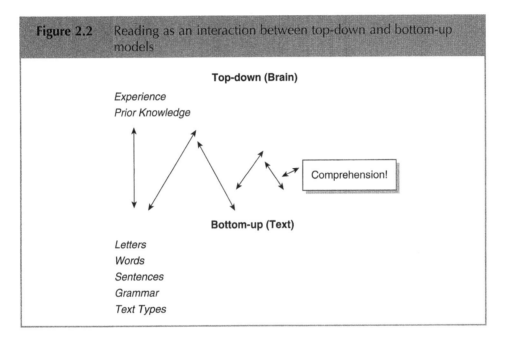

Figure 2.2 Reading as an interaction between top-down and bottom-up models

Figure 2.2 outlines the steps a fluent or mature reader may follow when reading a text using an interactive approach:

- *Hypothesize or predict:* Fluent readers try to predict what the text will be about. For example, when reading the newspaper, we know that a particular item is about sports because it is printed in the sports section. We use the headline to predict or guess what the article will be about and to determine if it interests us enough to continue reading.
- *Sample the text:* Fluent readers then look at important words that fit these guesses, but they don't look at function words such as *the* or *of*.
- *Cycle of sampling:* Fluent readers then enter a cycle of sampling until they can comprehend the meaning. If comprehension breaks down, a fluent reader will start the cycle all over again to see if he or she can comprehend the text on a second try.

- Which of the three models above best matches your philosophy of teaching reading and why?

DEFINITION OF READING

Up to now I have not offered any comprehensive definition of reading, so I invite you to write your definition of reading now that you have reflected on the reading process and the three different models of reading. After you have written your definition, compare it to the one I now present. One of the best definitions of reading that I have seen and that still holds true for me is the following:

> Reading is the process of constructing meaning through the dynamic interaction among the reader's existing knowledge, the information suggested by the written language, and the context of the reading situation. (Anthony, Pearson, & Raphael, 1993, p. 284)

This definition really sums up all of what I have presented so far about the reading process: Reading is not passive, as it involves the reader in *active* interaction with what is presented in the text in order to make sense of what is written.

IMPLICATIONS FOR TEACHING READING TO ELLs

Beginning ELL readers often are more focused on individual words (the bottom-up approach) than more fluent readers until they have built up a critical mass of language knowledge (Grabe, 1986). However, by relying only on the text for meaning, these beginning ELL readers may not always be able to successfully interpret the author's indented meaning. This is because the writer may have made certain assumptions about the background knowledge a reader would bring to the text. So teachers of reading to ELLs should remember the following points (all of which are discussed in greater detail in the chapters that follow) when preparing effective reading lessons (Farrell, 2002):

1. Readers bring something important to the text—previously acquired schemata. These schemata are networks of prior interpretations, and they become the basis for comprehension. The text is

filtered through these preexisting schemata, and readers will try to match these preexisting schemata with what they read in the text.

2. The meaning of the text is constructed by readers. Readers actively try to make connections between the text and what they already know about the world based on their cultural values, native language, and discourse processes.

3. The process of comprehension is a combination of top-down and bottom-up processes. When readers try to comprehend, there is a bouncing back-and-forth between readers and the text, between their top-down knowledge of the topic and the text. Comprehension is then reached, or, if it is not, readers will readjust until they do comprehend.

4. The teacher of reading should provide training in both the top-down and bottom-up processes. However, if the students are seen as stronger in one area, then compensatory instruction may need to be directed to the deficit area. For example, in order to enhance ELLs' bottom-up processing skills, teachers could provide word recognition exercises that encourage development of these automatic processes. Or to enhance ELLs' top-down processing skills, teachers could provide schema activation exercises (e.g., prediction activities) that encourage ELLs to access their prior knowledge of a topic.

CONCLUSION

This chapter started by asking teachers to reflect on reading and the reading process so that they could develop their own definition of reading that is based on an understanding of these processes and corresponding reading processing models. As a result of these reflections, teachers can consider that reading comprehension is probably accomplished by a combination of top-down and bottom-up processes. In other words, when ELLs try to comprehend a text, there is a bouncing back-and-forth effect between the reader and the text, between a reader's top-down knowledge of the topic and bottom-up knowledge of the written text. It is important for teachers to become aware of the reading process before they begin teaching reading. The chapters that follow outline and discuss various techniques that teachers can consider when teaching reading to ELLs.

3 Teaching Reading Fluency and Comprehension to ELLs

Most reading teachers have heard of the terms *fluency* and *comprehension*. We want to teach our students how to read for both. These are always good reasons for teaching reading, but sometimes we find that they can also be conflicting goals in our reading classes. On the one hand, we wonder how we can teach for reading fluency without checking our students' level of comprehension. Successful reading requires that readers not only decode the words in a text but also comprehend that text. But research has indicated that the effort expended to decode words in a text may actually compromise a reader's ability to comprehend that text. This chapter looks at both concepts; after you have read it, you should be able to make more informed choices about how to teach for both fluency and comprehension.

METACOGNITION

Before discussing the concepts of teaching reading for fluency and comprehension, I would like to emphasize that the contents of this book emphasize a strategic approach to reading. This means that we help our students become more aware of their own reading habits, good or bad, just as we reflected on our own reading processes in the previous chapter.

Strategic reading for ELLs has been defined as the "mental procedures that assist learning and that occasionally can be accompanied by overt activities" (Chamot & El-Dinary, 1999, p. 319) and involves teachers encouraging their students to become more aware of how they currently read. This has sometimes been called *metacognition,* or the "awareness and knowledge of one's mental processes such that one can monitor, regulate and direct them to a desired end" (Harris & Hodges, 1995, p. 153).

Teachers can instruct ELLs how to become more aware of their reading and then how to monitor their comprehension. For example, teachers can ask ELLs to rewrite the introduction and the ending of the text so that these are obviously not related to the main text or story. In this way, readers are alerted to the notion that if the text does not make sense, then something is wrong. One caution to note with this activity is that struggling readers may not realize or know when they do not understand, so teachers of struggling ELLs may want to explicitly show struggling readers how to monitor their own reading.

REFLECTION

- What does the concept *reading fluency* or *fluent reading* mean to you?
- How would you measure this fluency?
- What kind of activities do you think teachers should use in class to increase their students' reading fluency?
- Which is more important, reading fluency or reading comprehension, and why?

READING FLUENCY

Reading fluency means the ability to read accurately, quickly, effortlessly, and with appropriate expression and meaning (Rasinski, 2003). Reading fluency and reading competence are linked: It is important to know a student's reading fluency level, or the extent to which a student can achieve "seemingly effortless recognition of words in connected text" (Good, Simmons, & Kame'enui, 2001, p. 261), because it offers teachers the most reliable indicator of the student's reading competence (Kame'enui & Simmons, 2001).

Fluent readers are able to perform multiple tasks at the same time; for example, word recognition and comprehension—they can recognize words while also comprehending their meaning (Block & Israel, 2005). In addition, recent research in first language reading strongly suggests that reading instruction can make a difference and that each reader has the potential to become more fluent with correct intensive instruction. For example, recent brain research using functional magnetic resonance imaging (fMRI) has suggested that fluent readers use left hemisphere regions of the brain as they read. Shaywitz and colleagues (2004) have shown that when slow readers receive intensive reading instruction, they too show "increased activation in the left hemisphere regions" (p. 13). In addition, fluency training that combines previews and paired readings, extensive reading in class (i.e., Sustained Silent Reading), reading at home, and questions and discussions around readings can help students develop their reading abilities.

That said, the fluency versus comprehension debate will not go away, because research has also indicated that students who make few or no errors while they are reading (and we can assume are considered fluent, or can we?) but read very slowly have as little likelihood of comprehending what they read as students who read very quickly (McEwan, 2002). For ELLs the issue of fluency becomes even more clouded, because we are not sure if second/subsequent language reading problems are related to specific language problems (e.g., lack of vocabulary in the second language) or to specific reading problems (lack of reading skills in both the first and second languages). Koda (2005) has noted that both the reader's first language reading background and his or her proficiency level in the second language will significantly contribute to successful second language reading, because unlike beginning first language readers, ELLs can draw on their prior literacy experience.

Thus, it becomes even more important for teachers of ELLs to train their students to speed up reaction times and increase phonological awareness in order to increase reading fluency. Teachers can help their students increase their reading fluency by increasing their reading rates, but students should not speed up at the expense of accuracy. Indeed the opposite sometimes occurs in classes when teachers overemphasize accuracy when reading (as is reading aloud), and this impedes fluency. As Anderson (2003) maintains, when assisting ELLs with increasing their reading rates, the purpose is "not to develop *speed* readers, but *fluent* readers" (p. 76). Anderson (2003, p. 76) defines a fluent ELL reader as "one who reads at the rate of 200 words per-minute with at least 70 percent comprehension."

Reading fluency, as defined above, can also be achieved by getting students to read a lot of material in school at their own level of difficulty. However, reading at school is never enough, so students must also be encouraged to read voluntarily outside of school as well. (See Chapter 8, Promoting Extensive Reading for ELLs.) Glasgow and Farrell (2007) suggest that guided reading of instructional materials with emphasis on repeated reading of the same material is one of the most powerful ways to increase fluency (and even comprehension), and it transfers to other material not previously encountered. They suggest that meaningful expression can become important when reading poetry, scripts, oratory, and songs, which are meant to be preformed. In addition, Rasinski (2004) makes some good suggestions for authentic fluency instruction that requires repeated readings; practice or rehearsal of material such as songs, poetry, lyrics, plays, scripts, monologues, and other types of oral presentations work well for expressive oral reading and mastery of meaning.

REFLECTION

- What does reading comprehension mean to you?
- What kind of reading activities do you think teachers should use in class to increase their students' reading comprehension levels?

READING COMPREHENSION

The previous section suggests that being a fluent reader is a significant factor if one wants to experience "success" while reading; however, we also discovered that the term *success* means different things to different people (especially when it concerns ELLs), because one may read aloud "successfully" but not be able to comprehend what one is reading. Thus we teachers may be surprised to realize that reading fluency is in fact closely related to reading comprehension. Again, however, different interpretations of terms by different researchers influence our reflection and examination of the reading process.

The good news is that there is general agreement that as decoding becomes more automated (i.e., as reading becomes more fluent), readers are able to devote more attention to comprehending what they are reading. For our purposes, reading comprehension is basically the ELL's ability to construct meaning from the text through a combination of prior knowledge and previous experience with the topic, the information in the text, and the stance the reader takes in relationship to the text. Glasgow and Farrell (2006) suggest that think-alouds, that is, requiring readers to stop periodically in order to reflect on how they are processing and understanding the text and relate orally what reading strategies they are using (or failing to use), can remove the cloak of mystery surrounding reading comprehension for ELLs. Of course, readers vary in the type and amount of knowledge and skills they have; however, both *knowledge* and *skills* are very important when readers attempt to comprehend a text.

KNOWLEDGE

Knowledge includes background knowledge about the content and about the text itself. Koda (2005) has noted that there have been considerable efforts recently to "uncloak the mysteries of comprehension" for readers of second/subsequent languages. The most important characteristics of knowledge for ELLs is the extent of their world knowledge and how they are able to connect it, in order to make sense of it, with the text being read. This is achieved through a series of networkable connections known as *schema*, in which people organize their world knowledge into categories and systems that make retrieval easier (Pardo, 2004).

Schema theory recognizes that readers have prior knowledge about a topic before they read. This prior knowledge can be similar to what the reader encounters in a new text, and the similarity enables the reader to elaborate on the prior knowledge. Alternatively, the prior knowledge may be in conflict with the topic of the text, or the reader may have no prior knowledge of the topic. In these cases teachers can play a vital role in seeing that the readers' knowledge about the new topic is built up so that they can successfully comprehend a new text. Rumelhart (1980) has pointed out that schema theory suggests the text (written or spoken) does not by itself carry meaning. A text, therefore, only provides direction for readers as to how they should construct meaning that originates from their own background knowledge. These previously acquired knowledge structures are called, in the plural, *schemata*.

The implication for us as reading teachers, then, is that we should try to help our students relate textual materials to their background knowledge (see below for more details). Reading teachers can encourage this by trying to compare new input from a reading passage against some schema their students already have. All aspects of the previously existing schema must be compatible with the new input from the text. Anthony, Pearson, and Raphael (1993, p. 287) suggest that prior to reading lessons, teachers can "engage in activities designed to help students access or develop appropriate background knowledge." They also suggest that teachers ask students to apply their knowledge "as they generate predictions about the content" of the text they are about to read. The next chapter outlines various activities reading teachers can consider implementing before teaching a particular text so that they can activate their students' prior schema.

SKILLS

Skills include such things as basic language ability, decoding skills, and higher level thinking skills. Reading *skills* and reading *strategies* are not the same: Readers use their reading skills subconsciously, but they must consciously use specific reading strategies, which will be addressed in the section that follows. However, it takes time for ELLs to become skilled readers, and this is only accomplished by lots of reading repetition (Carrell, 1998). Thus, we can say that reading skills are processes that readers actually overlearn, because so much repetition guarantees both reading speed and accuracy.

Reading strategies, in contrast, are deliberate actions used by readers to achieve specific goals. (See the following chapter for details.) Reading skills draw on specific higher-order thinking skills in response to the demands of reading tasks; however, as we will see in the next chapter, teaching reading strategies is very different from teaching reading skills, which was the focus of much of the reading instruction of the 1960s and 1970s.

Beginning ELLs mainly use decoding skills while they read, whereas more fluent ELLs tend to use different skills, because they interact with the text itself (Koda, 2005). This interaction includes making inferences and hypothesizing *while* they are reading, and so reading skills can become reading strategies when they are used intentionally. Teachers can *teach* their struggling readers how to interact with the text by showing them how print relates to speech; specifically, in the beginning this means showing them how to extract phonological information from individual words. This is critical, because most words in beginning reader texts already are in the child's oral vocabulary. Koda (2005) suggests when teaching the basic decoding process to second/subsequent language readers, reading teachers stress that their students understand first how their own first language writing system works.

TEACHING READING FLUENCY AND COMPREHENSION TO ELLs

I put the *Teaching* in the above subheading on purpose, because in many reading classes worldwide, the majority of reading teachers tend to *test* rather than *teach* reading. Recent studies have found a common testing pattern in reading classes that includes reading aloud followed by comprehension questions that do not challenge readers. To increase reading comprehension levels of ELLs, teachers can teach both general and specific skills and also show their students how to apply these skills.

In general terms, teachers can build up their students' background knowledge so that the students can process the text they are reading more proficiently. One way teachers can do this is to provide a prereading summary of the text that introduces the story and outlines some of the vocabulary the ELLs will encounter. This summary can be prepared in as much detail as the teacher thinks the students may require. If an ELL's background knowledge of a topic is lacking, then reading teachers may have to preteach vocabulary specific to the text the students are reading. Graves (1984, pp. 246–247) suggests the following four ways teachers can select vocabulary specific to a student's knowledge of the text or topic:

1. *Type 1 words:* words that are in the students' oral vocabulary but that they cannot read.

2. *Type 2 words:* new meanings for words that are already in the students' reading vocabulary with one or more other meanings.

3. *Type 3 words:* words that are in neither the students' oral vocabulary nor their reading vocabulary and for which they do not have an available concept but for which a concept can be easily built.

4. *Type 4 words:* words that are in neither the students' oral vocabulary nor their reading vocabulary and for which they do not have an available concept or for which a concept cannot be easily built.

According to Graves (1984), teaching Type 3 and Type 4 words is the most time consuming for teachers of ELLs. In addition, teachers may want to consider using different word frequency lists to establish the four categories of words for their students. More ideas on how teachers can activate their students' background knowledge are discussed in Chapter 4, Teaching Reading Strategies to ELLs, and ideas for vocabulary development are discussed in Chapter 6, Teaching Vocabulary to ELLs.

Another general approach to increasing reading comprehension is to teach text structures explicitly. One of the more general ways to present this is to teach story grammars. A story grammar refers to the internal structure of a story, and research has indicated that story grammars are acquired when people continuously hear stories that contain these structures/grammars. For example, some texts are in narrative form, and ELLs can be made aware of that these stories usually follow the following structure: setting, event, complication, resolution.

REFLECTION

- Read the following story about *Dennis the Deer* and see if you can identify the structure of this story.

  Once upon a time there was a small deer named Dennis. He lived deep in the forest (1). One day, Dennis was wandering through the forest (2). Then he spotted a big mound of green grass in an open area (3). Dennis knew how delicious grass this green tasted (4). He wanted to taste it right away (5). So he walked slowly into the opening and bent down to eat the grass (6). Suddenly, Dennis saw a huge bear running at him (7). He was very frightened, so he ran and ran as fast as he could (8). Dennis will be more careful not to eat in the open again no matter how green the grass is (9).

Figure 3.1 below outlines the story structure (the parsing of the story), and you can see the numbers of the sentences under the relevant category.

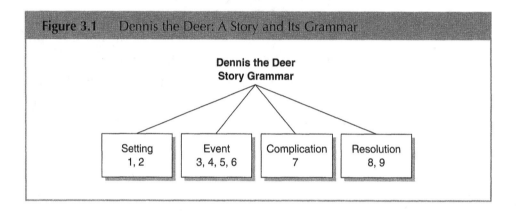

Figure 3.1 Dennis the Deer: A Story and Its Grammar

The story grammar has four main categories: setting, event, complication, and resolution. It is important to explicitly teach this type of story structure to ELLs, because as a text varies from culture, so does the notion of what represents an internal story structure. ELLs need to be able to understand a text's story structure if they are to be able to use the prediction skills and hypothesis testing that many fluent readers use naturally.

To increase reading comprehension levels, teachers of ELLs can also teach more specific skills, such as scaffolding, summarizing, and paraphrasing. For example, Clark and Graves (2005) describe different types of scaffolding, such as moment-to-moment verbal scaffolding and creating instructional frameworks that foster content learning. These may be useful for reading teachers to increase both reading comprehension and fluency. For moment-to-moment verbal scaffolding, the teacher prompts the students by asking probing questions.

In addition, Zygouris-Coe, Wiggins, and Smith (2004) suggest teachers model and provide opportunities for students to interact with the text as follows: Teachers ask students first to discuss three things they discovered from reading the text, then to discuss two interesting things they want to note as a result of reading the text, and then to ask one question they still have after reading the text. In order to do this, the teacher must first teach students how to summarize, that is, how to write a short, to-the-point outline of the main ideas in the text. When the students discuss two interesting things about the text they noted, teachers can encourage them to think about what they enjoyed most or what was most relevant to their everyday lives. Last, students write one question they still have about the text and this can also link the text to their everyday lives.

Fisk and Hurst (2003) suggest the following four steps for using paraphrasing to promote reading comprehension levels:

1. Initial silent reading, followed by some discussion to identify the main idea of the text.

2. A second reading, followed by note-taking to identify main ideas and supporting details.

3. After turning in copies of the text, writing a paraphrase relying on the notes.

4. Sharing the written paraphrase.

CONCLUSION

Most of the research on reading comprehension (e.g., Duke & Pearson, 2002) suggests that reading teachers should not only provide instruction that focuses specifically on comprehension processes such as predicting, looking for important information, and recognizing main ideas but also provide time for silent, teacher-monitored reading and opportunities to discuss the text. Research has also suggested that teachers teach readers when and how to use these comprehension processes (Block, Rodgers, & Johnson, 2004). In fact, Block and colleagues (2004) have pointed out that instruction for poor readers should be influenced by research on what expert readers do, such as setting a purpose for reading, becoming aware of and initiating their own comprehension processes, monitoring their own reading, making use of prior knowledge, using the text itself to make meaning, and making inferences. All of these comprehension processes are covered in the remaining chapters of this book.

4 Teaching Reading Strategies to ELLs

In the previous chapter, we noted that a major problem less skilled ELLs have while reading is that they do not often engage in comprehension monitoring. More proficient readers, on the other hand, constantly monitor their progress and will stop and take some action when comprehension breaks down. We also noted that reading skills and reading strategies are different: The former are more automatic and applied to the text unconsciously, while the latter are used purposely to achieve a particular reading goal. Anderson (2003) defines the difference by saying that strategies are "conscious actions that learners take to achieve desired goals or objectives, while a skill is a strategy that has become automated." This suggests that readers have an active role to play when engaging in strategic reading, because as they repeatedly practice and use particular reading strategies over time, the strategies become automated and thus turn into skills that are used subconsciously. The obvious conclusion is that less skilled readers can and should be taught how to use more effective reading strategies. This chapter outlines some of the reading strategies and activities that teachers of reading to ELLs can consider teaching.

REFLECTION

- What is your understanding of reading strategies?
- Do you use any strategies when you read?
- If you answered yes to the question above, list the strategies.

- If you are not sure, read a text and monitor your understanding as you read. Do you do anything specific to help you understand the text? For example, do you read each word for understanding, or do you read chunks of text for meaning?
- Do you think it is easy to teach reading strategies to students and that they can easily learn these strategies? Why or why not?

READING STRATEGIES

What/who is a good reader? According to Papalia (1987) more fluent readers use the following main strategies:

- Read things of interest
- Have knowledge about the topic
- Predict meaning
- Draw inferences from the title
- Skip words they do not know
- Guess the meaning of unknown words from the context
- Reread to check for comprehension
- Ask someone what a word means

So, research tells us that good readers distinguish between important information and less important details as they read, and they are able to use clues in the text to anticipate what information will come next and to relate new information to information already stated. They are also able to notice inconsistencies in a text and employ strategies to make these inconsistencies understandable. That said, it should also be noted that there are no "good" or "bad" reading strategies, because what is good for one reader (i.e., what makes him or her an efficient reader) may not work for another reader, and what is considered a "bad" reading strategy may actually work for some readers (Carrell, 1998).

As Carrell (1998) suggests, successful strategy use seems to depend on the context that the reading takes place in and the specific text students are reading. For reading teachers and ELLs, then, reading strategy training aims at improving the performance of struggling readers through explicit, step-by-step demonstrations of good reading behaviors that include instruction in metacognitive strategies (Koda, 2005). Some educators may think this type of instruction is present in most, if not all, ELL reading classes. However, research by Collins, Brown, and Holum (1991) has indicated that this is not the case and that in fact, in most classrooms (for readers in both first and second/subsequent languages), students do not practice strategic reading, because "the processes of thinking [about reading] are often invisible to both the students and the teacher" (p. 6). This is why we reflected previously on our own reading processes in Chapter 2, Reflecting on the Reading Process.

REFLECTION

- Here are some of these reading strategies that we have been referring to (adapted from Grabe & Stoller, 2002). No doubt you use all or most of these strategies yourself as you read. (If you are not sure, read a text and monitor your understanding as you read—do you do anything specific to help you understand the text? For example, do you read each word for understanding, or do you read chunks of text for meaning?)
  - o Predicting
  - o Using genre—knowing the nature of the text and using this knowledge to predict form or content
  - o Questioning
  - o Skimming—for gist or overview
  - o Scanning—looking rapidly for specific information
  - o Recognizing the topic in a text
  - o Classifying ideas into a main topic and supporting details
  - o Locating topic sentences—generalizing
  - o Stating the main idea of a sentence, paragraph, passage, or topic
  - o Recognizing patterns of relationships or ideas
  - o Identifying signal words such as *first, second,* and *then*
  - o Inferring the main idea
  - o Recognizing and using pronouns and referents—clues to cohesion
  - o Guessing the meaning of an unknown word from its context
  - o Paraphrasing—restating the text in your own words (to monitor comprehension)
  - o Summarizing—restating the main idea while leaving out details
  - o Drawing conclusions
  - o Drawing inferences and reading between the lines
  - o Visualizing what is described in the text
  - o Reading critically—distinguishing fact from opinion
- Explain each of the reading strategies above.
- How would you explain and teach these to ELL readers?
- Can you add more reading strategies?

TEACHING READING STRATEGIES TO ELLs

Strategic reading, according to Anderson (2003), means knowing not only what strategy to use from the above list but also when to use it, and reading teachers play an important role in getting this across to their students. Research suggests that reading strategies can and should be explicitly taught to ELLs and that when strategies are taught, students' performance on comprehension tests improves, and they are better able to recall the contents of a text. Paris, Wasik, and Turner (1991, p. 609), for example, have suggested six good reasons why we should teach reading strategies:

1. Strategies allow readers to elaborate upon, organize, and evaluate information derived from a text.

2. The acquisition of reading strategies coincides and overlaps with the development of multiple cognitive strategies to enhance attention, memory, communication, and learning.

3. Strategies are personal cognitive tools that can be used selectively and flexibly.

4. Strategic reading reflects metacognition and motivation, because readers need to have both the knowledge and disposition to use strategies.

5. Strategies that foster reading and thinking can be taught directly by teachers.

6. Strategic reading can enhance learning throughout the curriculum.

It is also important to remember that reading strategy instruction has as its chief goal improving the reading performance of ELLs. Teachers can accomplish this by modeling good reading behaviors for their students. Research also suggests that for reading strategy training to be effective, ELLs should first become aware of what strategies they currently use as they read. As Carrell (1998, p. 8) points out, "If learners are not aware of when comprehension is breaking down and what they can do about it, strategies introduced by the teacher will fail." Then and only then can ELLs begin to choose more appropriate strategies that will help them comprehend a text.

Teachers of reading to ELLs can consider the following four steps when introducing reading strategies to their students. The first three are adapted from Winograd and Hare (1988):

1. Explain *what* the strategy is: The teacher should describe what the strategy is.

2. Explain *why* a strategy should be learned: Students should be frequently reminded about the *benefits of the strategy* in order to effectively help them develop as successful readers.

3. *Model* the strategy for the students: Teachers should explain *how to use* the strategy effectively by modeling it. In other words, they should show the students how to do it.

I've added a fourth step:

4. *Follow up on the training:* Teaching reading strategies takes time; it can take several years for students to develop as effective and strategic readers (Farrell, 2005).

REFLECTION

- Have you ever attempted to teach reading strategies?
- If you have, were you successful? Which strategies were you successful with? Which strategies did not work? Why?

IMPLEMENTING READING STRATEGY INSTRUCTION

When teaching ELLs reading strategies, teachers should keep in mind that the goal of reading instruction is to develop strategic readers. Strategic readers do something *before* reading, *during* reading, and *after* reading.

BEFORE READING

In the previous chapter I mentioned that teachers could help students activate their students' schema about a text before the students read the text. I have found the following four activities useful when attempting to activate the relevant background schema of ELLs: *word association, direct experience, cinquain,* and *prediction* (Farrell, 2000, 2006).

Word Association

The rationale behind the word association task is to determine what prior knowledge students bring to a new topic before they read the text. It works as follows: Students respond (orally at first) to a key word or phrase such as "Sport is useful." Next, the students write down as many words or phrases as possible in three minutes that relate to this key phrase (e.g., sport is useful: healthy, expensive, fun, hard work, lose weight). The teacher then writes these words on the board. Alternatively, the students can be asked to free write on the topic. For this activity, students write everything they can think of about the topic for five minutes. While they are writing, the students should not worry about their grammar, spelling, or punctuation. The emphasis at this stage is on content, not accuracy in the language. From these exercises, teachers can use what they learn about their students' knowledge of the topic for their lesson planning.

Direct Experience

For this method, the students are required to get up from their seats and participate directly in some activity (such as a sport). The rationale behind the direct experience, or hands-on learning, is that students build on their background knowledge through firsthand experiences with concepts and vocabulary important to the lesson. Of course, the teacher must indicate which words or concepts are going to be important and write these on the board. This method requires the teacher to take the students through several steps and introduce a sport that may incite curiosity in the students. The following steps should be observed for this process, and the teacher should ensure the students go through the steps in the order they appear below:

- *Step 1*: Identify concepts important to the lesson.
- *Step 2*: Identify vocabulary that names those concepts.
- *Step 3*: Prepare a lesson that requires the students to directly participate in an activity that develops the concepts and uses the vocabulary.

For example, on the topic of sport, the following would be my outline:

- *Concepts:* self-development, character development, equality
- *Vocabulary:* excellence, pride, satisfaction, peak, instill, discipline, determination, open, neighborhood, enjoyment
- *New sport:* tae kwon do. All students should stand up and stretch their arms and legs. (This works especially well in afternoon classes.) They then sit and stretch. The students are then taken through various routines that are associated with tae kwon do. Thus, students get first-hand experience in a sport they are not likely to have experienced before. This also keeps attention focused on the lesson.

Cinquain

Another method that reading teachers can use to activate background knowledge is having the students write a cinquain. A cinquain is a five-line poem that reflects affective and cognitive responses to a concept (Shrum & Glisan, 1994). The rationale behind the cinquain is that it helps students develop prior knowledge for subsequent lessons in a poetic fashion. However, not many students will have experienced such a style of writing. Also, it is a challenging and creative activity.

A cinquain includes the following five lines, and the teacher should ensure the students write them in this order:

Line 1: one-word title

Line 2: two words that describe the title

Line 3: three words, each expressing an action

Line 4: four words, each expressing a feeling

Line 5: a different word for the title

For example, and again staying with the topic of sport, my cinquain would be as follows:

Sport

Have fun

Running, jumping, sliding

Laughing, shouting, crying, alive

Living

Prediction

Prediction is linked to the strategy of activating prior knowledge. Prediction creates anticipation and gets students thinking about previous experiences they may have had about the topic before they read about it. Prediction activity gets students to guess what will happen next in the story (from its title, headings, subheadings, photos, and pictures). Research has shown that good readers use prediction as they continue to read into a story by seeking to confirm or adjust their initial impression about the topic. So, prediction works both before and while reading. Prediction asks students to guess what will happen next in the story (from chapter headings and subheadings) and involves the readers in active interaction with the text by making them think about what they have read and what they will read next. The following steps may be useful for teachers of ELLs to consider when designing exercises and activities for prediction. (I thank my colleagues at the National Institute of Education, Singapore, for my understanding of these steps.)

- *Step 1:* Prepare a text and place it on the overhead projector or display it as a PowerPoint slide.
- *Step 2:* Show the students the title/picture/first line/first paragraph. Have the students predict what the text is about or what is going to happen next by asking questions such as, "What do you think this text will be about? Why? Can you support your answers?"

The purpose is not to get the correct answer but to encourage students to think about what they may read. Teachers can confirm or reject students' responses.

Prediction is a strategy used throughout the reading process (prereading, during reading, and postreading). Prereading activities include having the students guess what will come up in the lesson based on their prior experiences with the topic. During-reading prediction activities have the students using the text itself and any pictures or illustrations that confirm (or adjust) predictions made during prereading. Postreading prediction activities include having students make adjustments based on their reading of the text. At this post stage, the students confirm (or adjust) predictions made before they read. In this way, pre-, during- and postreading activities are linked together to give a coherent understanding of the text. (See below for specific examples.)

DURING READING

During-reading prediction procedures have the students using the text itself and any pictures or illustrations that confirm (or adjust) predictions made during reading. I will outline three (there are more, but research has indicated these three are the most important) such strategies that students can be taught to use while they are reading a text: prediction, questioning, and summarizing.

Prediction

One of the most interesting activities that I have used in my ELL reading classes and have encouraged in my teacher education courses is the directed reading teaching activity (DRTA) (Stauffer, 1969), which covers prereading, during-reading and postreading activities. The DRTA is intended to develop students' ability to read critically and reflectively. Broadly speaking, a DRTA lesson attempts to equip readers with the ability to determine their own purposes for reading and to examine reading material based upon these purposes. A typical DRTA lesson would progress as follows:

1. The teacher begins with a general introduction that also serves to check the students' background knowledge about the topic. This discussion not only orients the students to the topic but also increases their levels of motivation; since the teacher has now brought the topic to life, the students may want to learn more about it by reading the passage. At this opening stage of the DRTA lesson, it is the responsibility of the teacher to fill in any gaps in student knowledge about the topic. The teacher does not introduce vocabulary or set specific purposes for reading; rather, he or she encourages the students to make their own predictions about what they are going to read and to set their own purposes.

2. In the next phase of the DRTA lesson, students read the passage and determine if their initial predictions were correct. If the predictions were not correct, then the students need to adjust them (with the help of the teacher if necessary). The teacher can ask the students how accurate their predictions were. Additionally, as a way of monitoring the students' levels of success in their predictions, teachers can ask certain students to read aloud the sentences that confirmed their predictions. Also, the students may share what else they now know from reading the story.

3. In the final phase of a DRTA lesson, reading teachers design follow-up activities for students to check comprehension, discuss the topic, develop their vocabularies, and read and write critically.

Over the years however, many ELL reading teachers have interpreted this method in many different ways, so I will outline how I have used it in my teacher education courses. I use my own short story "What Goes Around, Comes Around!" (see Appendix at the end of this chapter) as a text. (You can use an easier text with your students depending on their proficiency levels.)

1. *DRTA Lesson Phase 1*: I ask the students what they think the words *what goes around, comes around* mean. I have gotten many answers, from giving back money that was loaned to taking revenge. When

I have decided that the students' schemas have been activated enough, I move onto Phase 2.

2. *DRTA Lesson Phase 2*: Now I distribute a copy of the first paragraph to each student and do prediction activation exercises with this first paragraph. (This first paragraph is reproduced in the Appendix at the end of this chapter.) For example, after the students read the first paragraph, I show them questions (either by displaying them on the overhead projector or by writing them on the blackboard) as follows:

- Title: "What Goes Around, Comes Around!"
  o What do you think this story is about? Why?
- John had been watching the two prison guards for two days now.
  o Who is John?
  o How do you know this?
- He both hated and feared them. There were many reasons for both.
  o Why do you think he hated them?
  o Why do you think he feared them?
- While he was a prisoner, these two guards were the most brutal when disciplining prisoners, and many had died from their beatings. He had not had much to do with these two particular guards, but before he escaped, he had heard enough from the other prisoners to know not to cross them in any way.
  o Which country do you think John is from? Why? What clues tell you that?
  o Why do you think John did not have experiences with these two prison guards before? How did he avoid them?
  o So far, do you think your prediction about the story based on the title is correct?
- Now both were on his trail, and so he purposely led them into an area of quicksand, an area he had grown up in and thus knew all too well.
  o What does this tell you may possibly happen? Why?

I then distribute each of the remaining paragraphs in sequence and do similar activities with each paragraph.

3. *DRTA Phase 3:* For the final phase of the lesson, I ask the students either to continue the story or to draw a sketch of the sequence of events in the story and to continue to sketch what they think may happen. I also ask some students to think about what went before the events of the first paragraph that makes this story what it is.

In this way reading teachers can encourage students to read between the lines as they predict what is to follow and avoid outright comprehension questions that test rather than teach reading. Other core reading strategies that should be included in the during-reading sessions are combinations of questioning, summarizing, organizing, and monitoring.

Questioning

Asking questions before reading and posing questions while reading are strategies that have been identified as being effective by fluent readers of English. Questions posed before reading encourage students to set a purpose for reading. These questions also guide the students as they read, and when they encounter passages or words that confuse them, they can ask themselves questions that help them understand. These questions during reading can be of these types: What is this paragraph about? Do I need to reread this? Are there words in the passage that confuse me? Asking questions after reading is also an effective reading strategy.

One idea would be to ask students to go back to the original questions they had before they started reading, and have them point out the ones they answered and the ones they were unable to answer. However, most of the time in a reading class the wrong people are asking most of the questions! The students are the ones who should be *asking*. For example, they can come up with *do-it-yourself questions:* Students can make up and answer their own questions. I have used the following method: Divide the class into groups. Ask each group to compose different types of questions about a passage (opinion, factual, and inferential questions). Have each group write possible answers for their questions. Then, ask the groups to exchange the questions *only* (not the answers as well), and have another group come up with possible answers. Also, ask them to try to identify what kind of question was asked (factual, opinion, or inferential). Have the groups compare their answers at the end. They can also attempt to predict what questions the teacher could ask on a quiz related to a text they are reading.

Summarizing

Summarization is a reading strategy used to get the gist of a text (McEwan, 2002). It is important that readers be able to get the main idea of a chunk of text, and summarizing can help as the reader restates the meaning in his or her own words. However, in order to teach this strategy effectively, McEwan (2002) suggests that teachers should locate chunks of text that do not introduce too many new and difficult words at once. Then summarizing can also improve students' recall of what they read and thus help their comprehension skills.

When teaching ELLs how to summarize what they have read, first show them how to recognize the topic sentence of each paragraph and where it is usually located (at the beginning of each paragraph), and then have them underline it. After this, have students delete unimportant information, such as all the examples of a topic. ELLs should skip information that is difficult and only return to it at the end if they still do not understand the passage.

Next, have students write all the topic sentences on a page and then try to join them all in fewer sentences. Depending on how long the summary is, then, students can begin to replace the actual words with their own words and rewrite the summary as many times as it takes to the desired length. Of course, teachers should first model this summarization technique with a passage for the whole class to follow, and they should think aloud to show how and why they decide to chunk a text and underline the main points.

REFLECTION

- Try to locate a suitable text for your students to read and teach them reading strategies using the three phases of a DRTA lesson outlined above.
- After you teach using the DRTA, next teach questioning and summarization strategies.

AFTER READING

When your students have finished reading a text, ask them to continue with the prediction exercises that they first attempted before they read the text. For example, after reading a text, the students may want to make changes to their initial predictions based on what they actually read in the text. At this postreading stage, the students are in a position where they can confirm (or adjust) their initial predictions, or they can see where they may have been taken by surprise by what they have read. In this way, *before, during,* and *after* reading activities are linked together to give a coherent understanding of the text as a whole. In addition, students can be asked to re-present the content of the text in an interesting and meaningful way. For example, if the text is one that tells a story, the students can re-present the story through drawings or through listing the events of the story.

CONCLUSION

Teaching reading strategies to ELLs is not an easy activity, because it takes time. As McEwan (2002) has noted, the process "will take far more than a day or two of casual staff development" (p. 77). However, there is sufficient proof from reading research that we should at least attempt to teach reading strategies to ELLs even if we realize that we should not expect immediate success. With repeated practice using reading strategies, there is a good chance that ELLs will be able to turn the reading strategies into reading skills as they continue to move from learning to read to reading to learn.

Appendix to Chapter 4

What Goes Around, Comes Around!

John had been watching the two prison guards for two days now. He both hated and feared them. There were many reasons for both. While he was a prisoner, these two guards were the most brutal when disciplining prisoners and many had died from their beatings. He had not had much to do with these two particular guards, but before he escaped, he had heard enough from the other prisoners to know not to cross them in any way. Now both were on his trail, and so he purposely led them into an area of quicksand, an area he had grown up in and thus knew all too well.

5 Teaching Text Structure to ELLs

Now that we have discussed reading strategies in the previous chapter, it is time to make a connection between reading strategies, reading purpose, and text types. Reading research has indicated that when ELLs are able to recognize different types of texts, they not only can better comprehend a text but they are also better able to recall information from that text after reading it (Carrell, 1985, 1992). In addition, when ELLs are able to recognize different language features within different types of texts (such as discourse markers), they are able to recall more information from each text later. Because ELLs can have such varied backgrounds in their first language, this chapter suggests that ESL readers need to be trained to recognize text organization in English for more effective reading comprehension.

In Chapter 3, Teaching Reading Fluency and Comprehension to ELLs, various models of reading were discussed that included a top-down approach, a bottom-up approach, and an interactive approach to reading. In each of these approaches, various aspects of text structure can be taught to ELLs in many different ways and research suggests that if ELLs can recognize different types of text, then the chances that they will be able to comprehend that text will also increase.

This chapter looks at texts first from a big-picture perspective and then from within that picture. We first look at how to recognize different text types and their schematic structure, and then we take a look within these texts to discuss how parts of a text are joined together with discourse markers. We also locate topics and main ideas of the text and consider how paragraphs are structured within that text. This follows from the previous chapter on strategies; teachers can and should explicitly teach deconstruction of texts in these ways so that they become reading strategies for beginning ELL readers. Research indicates that when these readers gain more insights into the makeup of the texts they are reading, these strategies can be transferred to their writing as well.

REFLECTION

- What is your understanding of text structure?
- How would you explain the different types of texts to ELLs?
- What is your understanding of discourse markers?
- How would you explain the different kinds of discourse markers in a text to ELLs?

TEXT STRUCTURE

There are of course many different types of written texts available to our students, and each has its own rules of what makes it such a text. For example, the main types of texts can be classified into fiction (novels, short stories, plays, and poetry) and nonfiction (essays, reports, and articles), but there are also other genres, such as letters, signs, messages and memos, and now text messages. Each of these has its own distinctive features that most fluent readers can identify. ELLs who are literate in their first language can identify many of the different genres, but some may need explicit instruction in the differences among genres. This is especially true for learners whose first language may have different genres than are usual in English.

So, the first and most general aspect of helping ELLs with different texts is to raise their awareness of the different features of each of these genres and how they can best comprehend each. That said, this chapter will first focus on how teachers of reading to ELLs can help develop awareness of text structures, especially top-level rhetorical organization of texts, regardless of the genre being read. This is because reading research has suggested that focused instruction that highlights the organization of texts may be beneficial for the development of ELLs' reading abilities.

Why this focus on rhetorical organization of texts? Well, in particular, because "explicit training about top-level rhetorical organization of texts" can greatly benefit comprehension and recall of text for ELLs (Carrell, 1992, p. 16). Ideally, teachers of reading to ELLs should provide a preview of the text and topic rather than only providing background knowledge or just asking students to read the text (Koda, 2005). In addition, research has shown that ELLs react positively to teacher-provided previews. They mention that they find the previews useful to aid their comprehension; this is important because teachers must consider student perception of what aids them as they read. The research suggests that previews offer promise because previewing provides support, especially if students encounter unfamiliar ideas and concepts in a text. Chapter 4, Teaching Reading Strategies to ELLs, has already touched upon the use of previewing and prediction with ELLs. This chapter will also include ideas for using previews to help ELLs better understand and recall texts.

Research suggests that if teachers provide a preview of the type of text the students are reading (compare/contrast, argumentation, cause/effect, etc.) and explain how the contents of that text are joined together, then readers are able to recall the contents more easily and effectively. The research further suggests that knowledge of these text structures is transferable to ELLs' writing development. Thus, students should be explicitly taught how to recognize the different types of texts. This will in turn lead them to be better able to identify the main ideas of the text and individual paragraphs. They will also be better able to distinguish between main ideas and supporting details and to understand how all the different parts of the text (opening paragraph, closing paragraph, discourse markers, and other text signposts) come together to make it a cohesive text (Koda, 2005).

TEXT TYPES

The following types of texts can be deconstructed by teachers and presented to students in diagram form so that students can recognize these and use deconstruction as a reading strategy. (I thank my colleagues at the National Institute of Education, Singapore, for information on the four text types.)

Type 1: Collection/Description

Here is an example of this simplest type, one that is used by very young children in story telling. (Note that the examples for Type 1 and Type 2 are on the same, using the topic, graduation.)

> Our school's Graduation Day was held late last year. It was held in the main gym of the school, because that is the only place we could get everybody together in one place. All the teachers, students, and parents turned up to see a variety of events take place. The senior students graduated, and some received prizes, while some junior students also received prizes for scholarship and sports achievements

during the school year. There was a lot of food to eat after the graduation ceremony and lots of sodas to drink. We all enjoyed the
Graduation Day.

A subset of collection is description. Description is "thing" oriented,
and under this we include examples and specifics concerning explana-
tions. It also includes the who, what, where, when, and why structure of
journalistic writing. Semantic mapping can also be used to schematically
represent this type of text organization as follows:

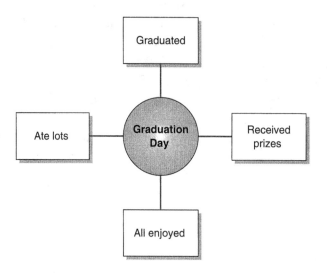

Type 2: Causation

Causation is another type of text structure, and one way of getting students to recognize *cause/effect* text types is by asking questions such as,
"What happens as a result of an action?" Teachers can explain the action,
such as, "I studied very hard every day for six months in preparation for
the graduation." This is a cause statement. The effect, or result, is what
happened as a result of the action, such as, "I graduated with honors."
Also, cause/effect relationships in texts are, for the most part, likely to be
single, or one-to-one. Here is another example (using the same story as
above, about graduation):

However, not all my student friends were able to graduate during that Graduation Ceremony. Mike, for example, wasn't studying well during the year because he had some health problems.
As a result, he was not able to attend many classes during the
year. His parents and his friends were very disappointed to see
this. They all hoped he would get better quickly and graduate
the next year.

Cause —————————————————▶ **Effect**

Mike was not healthy, did not attend classes.   *Mike failed to graduate.*
His parents and friends were
disappointed.

Type 3: Problem/Solution

The third text type is called problem/solution. Texts that present the reader with a problem usually include a solution or at least a proposed solution to the stated problem. In order to recognize this pattern, students should skim through the text after the problem has been stated and look for key words that outline some of the solutions. Unlike causation texts, problem/ solution texts include signal words, such as *first, second,* and *third,* or *one* followed later by *another,* that indicate time order. Here is an example:

These days many education experts are asking how teachers can do a better job teaching. With so much at stake in teaching, some education experts are speaking openly of replacing some bad teachers, because they make bad classroom decisions that can cause many problems for their future students' success. One solution may be to better educate teachers in their initial teacher education courses. Another solution would be to run more professional development courses after they have graduated.

Problem —————————————————▶ **Solution**

Some teachers make bad classroom decisions.   *Better initial teacher education*
The students' future suffers.   *Provide more professional*
development

Type 4: Compare/Contrast

The fourth text type addressed in this chapter is called compare/ contrast. When authors want to compare things, it usually means that they want to explain how these things are alike; however, when they want to explain how they are different, it means they want to contrast these things, as in the following example:

Today, many teachers are overworked and underappreciated, and some take substances such as increased amounts of caffeine to help them better cope with these stresses. Despite evidence that taking such substances may be harmful, many claim this is not so. In fact, many say they would not be able to continue without these, because the substances give them energy, and that they are harmless anyway.

View A ————————————————————→ Opposing View A

Taking caffeine is harmful.   *Caffeine may enhance performance.*

TECHNIQUES FOR DEVELOPING AWARENESS OF TEXT STRUCTURE

The following techniques can help students recognize different types of text structure (my thanks to Anthony Seow for showing me this idea):

- *Hierarchical summaries:* These are very useful for texts that have sections and subheadings. ELLs can work alone or in pairs or groups to first look at each section and then write the main point of each section (and supporting idea if time permits). After doing this for each section, they will have a summary of each section. Teachers and students can review the summaries together.
- *Concept maps:* These show relationships among concepts within a specific field of knowledge. After ELLs read the text, they write the main idea of the text (sometimes this will be the title) in the center of a page and usually in the center of a circle or oval (see example in the section on Collection/Description). Next, they draw several nodes or spokes that radiate out from that circle or oval to make it look like the hub of a bicycle wheel. The major topics associated with the main topic are attached to the end of each node/spoke, and then completed maps can be reviewed by the teacher and the students together.
- *Modified SQ3R strategy:* ELLs survey (S) the text, including headings and subheadings. They then read the first subheading and recite (R) it without looking at it. Next, they ask themselves questions (Q) about the subheading; then they reread (R) the subheading and recite (R) the important ideas in the section. They do the same for all the important ideas in each section.
- *Story maps:* These are useful with texts that have a story structure, such as setting—problem—goal—events—solution. Simply, the teacher asks ELLs questions that focus on this story structure so that they will eventually be able to identify this story structure themselves and use it later in their written work.

DISCOURSE MARKERS

In addition to recognizing text types as an aid to reading comprehension and recall, research has also indicated that successful readers use writers' signaling devices to help them understand texts. These signaling devices can be called discourse markers, and they are words and phrases that join parts of a text together just like the bands in a watch strap—without them, the watch will fall off your wrist. If teachers can *teach* their students to become more aware of such devices, the students can better understand the text and as a result may be better able to use these discourse markers in their own writing. Figure 5.1 lists some of these discourse markers together with their functions.

Figure 5.1 Discourse markers	
Marker	**Function**
first, second, third . . . last	• To make a list
furthermore, moreover, what is more	• To add more to a list a
but, however, although	• To make a contrast
in order to, so that, so	• To state the purpose
as a result, consequently, therefore	• To explain a result
then, next, later, after a while	• To note a sequence o
finally, in conclusion, to sum up	• To sum up

REFLECTION

- Can you add to the list of discourse markers above?
- How would you teach discourse markers?
- Would you give your student the list of discourse markers above? If you would, how would you suggest they use it?
- Compare your answers with what you read below.

Some of the most common ways of teaching discourse markers are by providing a list of them (such as that in Figure 5.1) and by having students underline them in a text they are reading in an *identification* type of activity. There is nothing wrong with these activities, but if these are the only activities used, students may not fully understand not only how to recognize discourse markers but also how to use them in their own writing. Thus, teachers may want to consider *application* activities to use after students have mastered identification of discourse markers.

There are two types of application activities that teachers can use with discourse markers: (1) fill-in-the-blank activities, where students fill in the blanks with appropriate discourse markers; and (2) location activities, where students locate discourse markers in a text without any blanks. Here the teacher erases all the discourse markers from a text but does not leave any blanks (and thus does not alert students that discourse markers should be applied), so the students must locate places in the text where they think it most appropriate to place discourse markers. Of course, Type 1 application activities are easier than Type 2, because in order to complete Type 2 exercises, the students must be able to determine that a discourse marker is missing (there is no blank to alert them) and then be able to tell which one is missing. I would suggest that teachers move from identification to application Type 1 exercises before moving on to the more difficult application Type 2 exercises when their students are more proficient.

IDENTIFYING TOPICS AND MAIN IDEAS

As we have pointed out in previous chapters, some reading classes consist of students reading a text of some kind and answering comprehension questions at the end of that text. Many of these comprehension questions ask readers to locate the main idea of a passage or paragraph. Mikulecky (1990) suggests that readers practice these skills in a developmental sequence from simple to more complex cognitive tasks. For example, the sequence of exercises should include recognizing the topic of a paragraph first, and then identifying the main idea of a passage, as described in the next two sections.

Recognizing the Topic of a Paragraph

A paragraph is a group of sentences that collectively help develop a central point. In many cases the central idea of a paragraph is contained in the topic sentence, which usually (but not always) appears at the beginning of the paragraph. Have students read the paragraph that follows (from Mikulecky, 1990, p. 99) and identify the sentence that does not belong in it. Ask them to cross out that sentence and explain why it does not belong, and then to write the topic of the paragraph. When you have finished, create more exercises that practice recognizing the topic of a paragraph.

The Los Angeles Lakers are a championship basketball team. Their home court is the Forum, a modern stadium near Hollywood, California, and among their fans are some of the biggest names in the entertainment industry. Most basketball teams are based in large cities. Whenever the Lakers play at home games, they can be sure that stars like Jack Nicholson and Johnny Carson will be there to cheer for them. They have won four championships in the past eight years.

Topic: _____

Identifying the Main Idea of a Passage

As stated above, the main idea of a paragraph is sometimes stated in the topic sentence of a paragraph. However, recognizing the main idea of a passage consisting of multiple paragraphs with multiple topic sentences is more challenging. In this case, readers may have to rely on a combination of many strategies: predicting, prior knowledge, knowledge of text structure, skimming, scanning, and recognizing topic sentences.

Ask students to read the passage below, from which the title has been purposely omitted. Then ask them to answer these questions: What would an appropriate title be? What is the main point of the passage? What is the main idea of the first paragraph? What is the main idea of the second paragraph? Now develop further passages and exercises that have students developing this strategy of identifying the main idea of a passage or paragraph.

Running is not a new sport. People were doing it hundreds of years ago. These days many people run or jog each day as part of their exercise routine. However, some people run in races as their profession. These athletes have to be in very good shape physically in order to run these races. Runners know a good diet is important for their training. They try to eat very healthy foods, especially before a race. Every year, there are many long races in many parts of the world. One of the most famous of these races is held in Boston in the United States of America.

The Boston race is called the Boston Marathon. This is one of the oldest races in the United States. In 1985, more than 6,000 people ran in the Boston Marathon. They came from all over the world. In some races, the winners get large amounts of money. But for almost one hundred years, they got no money at all in the Boston Marathon. Recently, the winners were awarded prize money.

[My answers would be: Title: *Running*. Main point: *running as a profession*. First paragraph: *training to run professionally*. Second paragraph: *Boston marathon*]

USE OF QUESTIONS

Questioning as a means of previewing a text is another important strategy that proficient readers use. Fluent readers of English identify asking questions before reading and posing questions while reading as effective strategies for comprehension. Questions posed before reading encourage students to set a purpose for reading as ELLs preview the text. These questions also aid ELLs' comprehension as they read and when they meet some passages and/or words that confuse them. Examples of appropriate questions include the following: What is this paragraph about? Do I need to reread this? Are there words in the passage that confuse me? Teachers can also use "do-it-yourself questions" where the learners compose (and answer) their own questions before reading the text. In another previewing activity I call "preface," learners suggest what might have happened before.

REFLECTION

- Look at the story in Chapter 4, "What Goes Around, Comes Around!" Tell the story from the time before John escaped from the prison.

Of course, asking questions after reading is also an effective reading strategy. One idea is to ask students to go back to the preview questions they had before they started reading and have them point out the ones they answered and the ones they were unable to answer. This strategy is connected to the KWL strategy outlined in Chapter 7, Planning Effective Reading Lessons for ELLs. Questions that encourage students to establish a personal connection to the text are also useful. Ask students to (1) find a passage in a story that was particularly meaningful for them, (2) explain any similar experiences they have had, and (3) explain how they relate to a character of the story or how they have been affected by the story. Teachers can model the writing of these questions.

ELL reading teachers can also develop "gapped text" exercises. Throughout the text or toward the end, teachers create a number of gaps that can be filled in only by readers who have understood the text up to that point. (Note, though, that this is different from the conventional cloze test, a test with regular gaps throughout that assesses grammatical and lexical accuracy and actually discourages purposeful, fluent reading.) Another activity ELL teachers can use when teaching text structure is to create mistakes in a text, such as inserting incorrect words, omitting key paragraphs, or omitting the beginning or ending of a story. Tell learners how many mistakes to look for but not necessarily which ones. After practicing this, students can then take a text and create their own "mistakes" to be discovered by other groups of students in the class.

RECIPROCAL TEACHING AND TEXT STRUCTURE

Reciprocal teaching is an instructional activity where the teacher and his or her students discuss segments of text while taking turns using the following four strategies: summarizing, question generating, clarifying, and predicting (Palincsar, 1986). The group brings meaning to the text using each strategy. Summarizing provides opportunities to integrate the most important information in the text. Students start by summarizing at sentence and paragraph levels, and later, as the reciprocal teaching continues, they can move to summarizing whole passages. Just as outlined above, when students generate their own questions after identifying relevant information, they can also answer these questions.

Reciprocal teaching also allows ELLs to clarify meaning, and any difficulties with comprehension can be identified and discussed. This can be aided with prediction exercises, where students are asked what will occur next in the text. When incorporating reciprocal teaching into a class on text structures for ELLs, teachers can first have their students read silently and then ask them comprehension questions about the text, making sure all questions are related to the specific strategies (like the ones outlined above). Next the teacher models how a student teacher would learn to teach using the strategy, so that the class learns about the process of teaching. Finally, a student "teacher" can take over and ask comprehension questions of his or her peers on a given text. So reciprocal teaching can aid ELLs when they attempt to construct meaning from a sentence, paragraph, or whole passage, while at the same time teachers can monitor how they are reading so that they can be shown effective strategies.

CONCLUSION

This chapter focused on teaching text structure and teaching discourse markers: the "big picture" of the text and the nuts and bolts that keep it together, much like the bands of a watch strap. Teaching students to recognize the different types of texts and discourse markers helps them better comprehend and recall the contents of a text while at the same time contributing to a greater mastery of writing skills.

6 Teaching Vocabulary to ELLs

In the previous chapter we noted that ELLs who were explicitly taught how to recognize structures in a text generally tended to comprehend that text as well. In order to be able to recognize a text, however, ELLs must also know at least 98 percent of the words in that text, and this is probably the vocabulary threshold below which comprehension may be unlikely. In addition, a large vocabulary is critical not only for our ELLs' reading purposes but also for all other language skills such as speaking, writing, and listening comprehension (Grabe & Stoller, 2002). Thus, a large vocabulary is seen by many as the key to comprehending a text; in other words, the more words a reader knows, the more text the reader will understand. This chapter outlines how teachers of reading to ELLs can explicitly *teach* (rather than test) various strategies so that our students can enlarge their word banks.

REFLECTION

- What is your understanding of the term *vocabulary?*
- How do you think students learn new vocabulary?
- How do you or would you teach vocabulary?

DEFINING VOCABULARY

A "word," as Hunt and Beglar (2002, p. 258) note, includes "its base form (e.g., *make*) and its inflections and derivatives (e.g., *makes, made, making, maker, and makers*)." In addition, words may include prefixes (*un-, co-*), and suffixes (*-tion, -ing*). Research has indicated that people store words semantically, not alphabetically like in a dictionary; that the more we use a word, the easier it is to remember; and that we will remember faster the words we have more recently used. Many times we teachers suggest that our students read as much as they can so that they can expand their vocabularies.

We can hope this happens, and sometimes it does, but we teachers too have an important role to play in motivating our students to enlarge their vocabulary banks (Nation, 2002) by intervening directly and *teaching* them how to do this. Many teachers try to accomplish this by getting their students to memorize word lists or look at synonyms and antonyms of a word and then doing fill-in-the-blank exercises connected to these memorized words. These efforts may be useful, but recent research has indicated that ELLs acquire vocabulary more effectively when they are directly involved in constructing meaning of the word rather than when they memorize definitions or synonyms (Koda, 2005).

PRINCIPLES OF *TEACHING* VOCABULARY TO ELLs

The following set of guiding principles can be applied by reading teachers of ELLs in a variety of teaching and learning situations (adapted from Nation, 2003, pp. 135–140).

1. Focus on the most-useful vocabulary first.

The most-useful vocabulary is the, 1,000 most frequent word families of English (see Nation, 2002, for a complete general word list), because this list includes almost 75 percent of common words in newspapers, academic texts, and novels as well as about 85 percent of words commonly used in conversation. It contains many of the 176 families of function words (words such as a, the, of, because, and could that are not nouns, verbs, adjectives, or adverbs).

After they have mastered the most-useful vocabulary, other words they should learn depend on the goals of the learners. English contains 120,000 low-frequency words, but these are best learned after high-frequency words. In addition to teaching general words, which are the main focus of the definition and this chapter, teachers may also want to consider teaching ELLs academic vocabulary or words that are common to academic discipline but are not in the most-useful vocabulary list. Teachers wishing to teach these particular words should view Coxhead's (2000) Academic Word List (AWL) of 570 word families.

2. Focus on the vocabulary in the most appropriate way.

After looking at what words to teach, teachers of reading to ELLs should consider how to teach these words, and the remainder of this chapter considers many of strategies for this purpose. Nation (2003) again suggests that teachers of ELLs use actual classroom time to directly and explicitly teach high-frequency words by

- having ELLs read and listen to others read graded readers containing these words (many publishing companies have many such graded readers available for ELLs),
- having them study the words and do exercises based on them, and
- having them speak and write using these high-frequency words.

3. Give attention to the high-frequency words across the four strands of an English language course.

Teachers of reading to ELLs need to ensure that the high-frequency words occur in a deliberate manner through teaching and study and are used in listening, speaking, reading, and writing lessons. These high-frequency words consist of 2,000 word families that include 176 function words and account for 80 to 95 percent of words in running text (Nation, 2002).

4. Encourage ELLs to reflect on and take responsibility for learning.

Our students need to realize that they must be responsible for their own learning. Taking this responsibility requires knowing what to learn, knowing the range of options for learning vocabulary, skill in choosing the best options, and the ability to monitor and evaluate progress with those options.

ANALYZING VOCABULARY

This section talks about how we can help our ELLs analyze vocabulary in different ways while at the same time taking the above principles into consideration. Teachers of reading to ELLs can begin at the word level by providing different activities related to the make-up of a word and by using word games and word-recognition exercises.

Analyzing Words

Every word has a base called a *root* or *stem* that is its smallest unit of meaning. Aebersold and Field (1997, p. 144) suggest the following set of procedures to analyze parts of words:

1. Ask ELLs to look at a certain word and divide it into its parts. Tell them to look for familiar prefixes (word parts that precede the base and add meaning), bases, and suffixes (word parts that follow the base).

2. Ask them what the base is and what it means. If they are uncertain about whether a part is a base or not, ask them to think of other words they know that have the same part.

3. If there is a prefix, ask them what it means.

4. If there is a suffix, ask what its grammar function is.

5. Have students check the meaning they have come up with to see if it fits the context of the sentence(s) they are reading. Can they think of a synonym with the same meaning?

Teaching the skill of analyzing words can be part of regular instruction while reading a text. Teachers can go through the above steps quickly as a way of reminding the ELLs of the steps and what they are for, so the students can use the steps when reading on their own.

Word Recognition Activities

Teachers of reading to ELLs can also include various fluency-building techniques that recycle already known words so that their students can recognize or use these words without much hesitation. One clear goal of reading instruction, especially for beginning ELLs, is to provide activities that enhance students' bottom-up reading skills (see Chapter 2, Reflecting on the Reading Process, for an explanation of this), and this can be accomplished by using word recognition exercises that encourage development of automatic processes. Although this is not really a reading strategy, the purpose of word recognition exercises is to improve our ELLs' ability to focus quickly on words for instant recognition and understanding.

The following four exercises are just some of the choices reading teachers have to encourage students to recognize words quickly. Of course teachers can develop their own activities that suit their particular contexts and student needs. It's important to note here that teachers should time these exercises; they should not be carried out so slowly as to allow students to sound out each word. Moreover, if the exercises are carried out too slowly, then the students may lose interest in the activity.

Example 1. Word-Recognition Exercise: Same Words

Directions: Read these words quickly and mark all the words in each line that are the same as the first word in the line.

some	some	sum	sold	smell	some
hope	hop	home	hole	hope	hold
tried	try	tired	tree	three	tried

Example 2. Word-Recognition Exercise: Synonyms

Directions: Read these words quickly and mark all the words in each line that have the same meaning as or a similar meaning to the first word in the line.

happy	glad	angry	hungry	content	pretty
begin	start	believe	gain	earn	commence
sick	slick	ill	angry	lazy	sore

Example 3. Word-Recognition Exercise: Antonyms

Directions: Read these words quickly and mark all the words in each line that mean the opposite of the first word in the line.

sweet	good	sour	lemon	sugar	tall
climb	march	fall	shave	sing	lower
cheap	small	bright	natural	expensive	pretty

Example 4. Word-Recognition Exercise: Unrelated Words

Directions: Read these words quickly and mark all the words in each line that are not in any way related to the first word in the line.

bed	sleep	sick	tired	bedroom	milk
school	pupils	dog	teachers	boats	chalk
travel	ship	plane	hotel	finger	lunch

Word Games

To make learning words fun, interactive, and empowering, teachers can also use various vocabulary games. For example, the following game that can teach word formation is called *Kangaroo Words* or *Words Within Words* (I am not sure of the exact reference for this game, so I apologize for not giving credit to the individual who first used it). Ask students to look at the words and find words within the word that mean *exactly* the same as the original word. Tell them that they may erase letters in each word but they may not rearrange any of the letters. The following is a short list of such words:

Main Word	Shorter Word
perimeter	rim
indolent	idle
encourage	urge
prosecute	sue
container	can
rampage	rage
curtail	cut
masculine	male

Analyzing Words in Context

Another main goal of explicitly teaching vocabulary is to help students deal with unfamiliar words when a teacher is not nearby to help, such as when they are reading alone at home. Of course, they can use a dictionary; however, a dictionary will not give the meaning of the word in different contexts. One way of helping them cope with unfamiliar words is to teach them how to guess word meanings in context. Nation and Coady (1988, pp. 104–105) suggest the following five-steps for this purpose:

1. Determine the part of speech of the unknown word.

2. Look at the immediate context and simplify if necessary.

3. Look at the wider context. This entails examining the clause with the unknown word and its relationship to the surrounding clauses and sentences.

4. Guess the meaning of the unknown word.

5. Check that the guess is correct.

The above procedures can also be used together with the following ideas for helping our ELLs guess the meaning of unknown words:

- *Contrast:* The word means the *opposite* of another word or expression in the text. *Example:* A frugal boss will never give a generous bonus at the end of the year. (*Frugal* is the opposite of *generous.*)
- *Cause:* The word is the cause of something described in the text. *Example:* Anorexia is a disease associated with many deaths in young girls because they want to lose too much weight. (*Anorexia* means *weight loss leading to death.*)
- *Consequence:* The word is used to describe the result of something. *Example:* Lung cancer can result from too much smoking. (*Cancer* is the result of *smoking.*)
- *Explanation:* The meaning of the word is explained, a definition is given, or an example is given. *Example:* Kimchee, a Korean fermented cabbage, is a very delicious food. (*Fermented cabbage* is the definition of *kimchee.*)
- *Hyponyms:* A reader may be able to see the relationship between a familiar word and an unfamiliar one by looking at the general word class such as *boat, ship, tanker, supertanker* where boat is used as a *hyponym. Example:* We must prevent oil spills from supertankers. An example took place in 1970 near Spain when an oil spill from a wrecked tanker exploded into fire. These types of ships are difficult to control in busy waters. (A *supertanker* is a *tanker,* which is a *ship.*)
- *Definition:* Definitions of words may sometimes be found in the text. *Example:* Neuralgia, a sharp, violent pain along a nerve pathway, can be treated with aspirin. (*Neuralgia* is *nerve pain.*)
- *Punctuation:* Readers can use the punctuation in the sentence to figure out the meaning of the word they do not know. For example, readers can use such clues as italics (showing how a word is defined), quotation marks (showing the word has special meaning), dashes (showing apposition, definitions), and brackets (enclosing a definition). *Example:* tae kwon do—a Korean martial art—is very good for self-defense. (The *meaning is between the two dashes.*)
- *Inference:* Contexts give examples from which a reader can infer the meaning of a term. *Example:* The misogynist manager disliked all the women in his office, so they all resigned. (A *misogynist* is a *woman hater.*)

THE VOCABULARY LESSON

Aebersold and Field (1997) suggest that teachers of ELLs consider the time sequence of a lesson that focuses on vocabulary building (once the text has been selected) by deciding on the vocabulary to teach *before* reading the text, *during* reading, and *after* reading the text. When considering the words to teach before reading, they suggest teachers first consider what words the students already know, what words they need to know to comprehend the text, and what words they will need to know to "function in the L2/FL in the future" (Aebersold & Field, 1997, p. 139).

They call words that appear frequently in the text and that are related to the topic *content-specific vocabulary,* and they maintain that these should be explicitly taught before reading the text. They note that during reading ELLs will encounter some words they have never seen before and so must be taught strategies to guess these words' meaning (like the strategies outlined in the previous section). When teaching students how to use these strategies, it is important for teachers to model their use by thinking aloud as they attempt to guess the meaning of words.

After the students have read the text, the teacher should revisit vocabulary in order to reinforce vocabulary skills and retention, especially of words that were deemed important for the ELLs' future linguistics development. Regarding the latter, Aebersold and Field (1997) say that teachers of reading to ELLs can individualize vocabulary development by getting the students to use word cards as they read by themselves. However, they note that creating such cards takes time and care and so should only be used for a limited number of high-frequency words that the ELL is interested in learning. To create a word card, ELLs write the word on the front of the card along with its pronunciation, any related family words, and (at the bottom of the front side) the sentence containing the word from the original text. On the back of the card, ELLs write a definition of the word, its part of speech (verb, noun), and its synonyms, if any, along with their own sentences using the word. Aebersold and Field (1997, p. 152) suggest that teachers then use the following steps for reviewing the word cards:

- *Step 1:* Students should look at the word, its pronunciation, and the related family words on the front of the card to see if they can recall the definition.
- *Step 2:* If they think they know the definition, they should turn the card over and check.
- *Step 3:* If they cannot recall the definition, they should look at the sentence in which they found the word on the bottom of the front card. If they can then give a definition, they should turn the card over and check it.

- *Step 4:* If they cannot come up with a definition, they should turn the card over and read the definition and the sentence they wrote on their own using that word on the back of the card.
- *Step 5:* After they learn the word, the card can be removed from the "to learn" pile and put in the "to review from time to time" file.

Teaching Unfamiliar Words

The following ideas (adapted from Hunt & Beglar, 2002, pp. 260–261) can be taken into consideration when teaching vocabulary that is unfamiliar to ELLs:

1. ELLs need to do more than just see the form of a word. They also need to hear the pronunciation and practice saying the word aloud as well. The syllable structure and stress pattern of the word are important, because these are two ways in which words are stored in memory.

2. ELLs should start by learning semantically unrelated words and also avoid learning words with similar forms and closely related meanings at the same time. For example, because *affect* and *effect* have similar forms, simultaneously studying them is likely to cause confusion.

3. It is more effective to study words regularly over several short sessions than to study them for one or two longer sessions. As most forgetting occurs immediately after initial exposure to the word, repetition and review should take place almost immediately after studying a word for the first time.

4. ELLs should study five to seven words at a time, dividing larger numbers of words into smaller groups.

Regarding the first item in the above list, teachers of reading to ELLs should realize that in the early primary-grade classrooms, word recognition presents a significant challenge for all our students. This is because as they work to construct meaning, they must also allocate great attention to activating and applying their developing knowledge of word recognition strategies. Consequently, teachers of reading to ELLs may first want to focus their students' attention on graphophonic knowledge and word-part identification strategies. Asking them to identify graphemes and phonemes directs them to consider individual letters and sounds For example, a teacher might explain, "It is a soft *c*," or "The *y* is acting like an *i*" or ask, "Does the *-or* sound like *–or* in corn or in actor?

In addition, Nation (2002, p. 30) provides the following five-step strategy that teachers can use to train ELLs to give attention to the context that surrounds unfamiliar words:

1. Look at the unknown word and decide what part of speech it is (noun, verb, etc.).

2. Look at the immediate context of the word and how it relates to other words around it.

3. Look at the clause the word is in and how it relates to other clauses around it.

4. Guess the meaning of the word.

5. Check whether your guess is correct.

CONCLUSION

This chapter has outlined various different methods that teachers of reading to ELLs can choose, depending on their students' needs, to teach vocabulary. The methods and activities presented in this chapter are designed to encourage our students to become independent readers, so if they encounter a word or words they have never seen before, they do not give up; rather, they can make an intelligent guess as to its meaning. In addition, it may be best for teachers of reading to ELLs not to simply assume that students from different first language backgrounds will carry out reading processes in the same ways, and this will need to be researched much more in the future (Koda, 2005).

7 Planning Effective Reading Lessons for ELLs

In the preceding chapters we considered the nature of reading and the reading processes. We should now think about how to plan effective reading lessons. Reading lesson plans, or systemic records of a teacher's thoughts about what will be covered during a lesson (Farrell, 2002), help us to think about the lesson in advance and to "resolve problems and difficulties, to provide a structure for a lesson, to provide a 'map' for the teacher to follow, and to provide a record of what has been taught" (Richards, 1998, p. 103). This chapter covers various issues we need to consider when planning effective reading lessons.

READING LESSONS

In her early research, Au (1980) discovered that ELLs who are from minority groups in Hawaii may have a different notion of classroom rules for interaction (especially rules for participation) than children from the majority culture have. For these learners, she discovered that there was some discontinuity between the language interaction patterns of the home and those of the school, and this discontinuity, or set of rule differences, decreased the rate of minority student interaction with the teachers. Based on these findings, she developed the Kamehameha Early Education Program (KEEP), an intervention program for minority ELLs that was designed to maximize the students' own cultural knowledge and use of language while at the same time developing their interactional competencies to be able to successfully participate in classroom reading events. Creating a program with instructional practices similar to the cultural interactional patterns of the Hawaiian children called for the following changes to standard classroom organization:

- The classroom was organized into smaller learning centers.
- The students self-selected when to work with other students and which other students they would work with.
- Direct instruction lasted 20 minutes only and was followed by storytelling, in which two or more people co-narrated a story, as is common in the Hawaiian culture.

These results have implications for teachers of reading to ELLs, as we should remember that our students who come from different first language backgrounds may be functioning with different notions and rules about appropriate classroom interaction and about participation in reading classes in particular. It is up to us as teachers to make our students aware of the rules of classroom interaction. We can do this by modeling the behavior we expect and then asking our ELLs to compare this with what they may have experienced in their own culture. This is especially important if the ELLs' culture is greatly different from the culture in which we are teaching them, where we tend to teach reading as follows:

1. We have students read a text.

2. We then discuss the text.

3. We ask questions during the discussions; sometimes we ask questions of the class, and sometimes we ask questions of an individual student by calling the name of that student.

4. When we ask questions of the group, we may have rules for responding. Commonly, we require students to raise their hands and not shout out the answers; then we choose a particular student to answer. No other student may answer at this time.

5. When we ask questions of an individual student by name, no other student may shout out the answer.

For many teachers of reading, these points may seem obvious, but they are not so obvious to many of our ELLs. For example, Susan Philips (1972) compared verbal interaction in Anglo-American classrooms with that of those in the Warm Springs Indian Reservation community. She discovered that in most Anglo classrooms, normal verbal interaction fell into one of four participant structures, with the first two being most common:

1. The teacher interacts with all students (this is most common) and controls who will talk and when.

2. The teacher interacts with small groups of students such as reading groups (also common), where student participation is generally the result of the teacher recognizing a particular student as speaker.

3. Students work individually at their desks, and the teacher is available for student-initiated interaction.

4. Small groups of students work together to complete specific tasks or projects with indirect supervision by the teacher. This is common only in the higher grades.

However, when she observed the Warm Springs children's participation in classrooms, she noted that the students in Warm Springs classrooms were less willing to participate verbally when asked to speak alone or in front of other students, when called upon by teacher, and when asked to take a leadership role. But, she discovered that they were more willing to participate in whole-group activities and when they could self-select when to speak.

Perhaps teachers of reading to ELLs can conduct action research into students' background cultures, their first languages, and the verbal interaction patterns in those languages as well as their students' learning styles so that they can develop strategies to manage and balance the interaction in their reading classes. The following principles may also be helpful for teachers of reading to ELLs to consider when designing effective reading classes.

PRINCIPLES FOR DESIGNING EFFECTIVE READING LESSONS FOR ELLs

One of the most important concerns for teachers is how to make their classes interesting and relevant for their students. This is not an easy concern to address, because our students have such diverse interests, and it would be impossible to choose materials that would satisfy everybody. Of course, choosing a correct reading text depends on the goals of the reading course. Consequently, teachers may want to focus on these goals when choosing suitable reading materials. One interesting way to do this is to let students choose their own materials (see Chapter 8, Promoting Extensive Reading for ELLs, for more ideas on this topic). However, this may be difficult, as many programs may have prescribed materials and texts and teachers have to use these materials regardless of their students' preferences. The following principles (adapted from Richards, 1990) may be useful for teachers to follow when developing lesson plans for a reading class:

1. Use reading materials that are interesting.

With modern technology and the Internet in particular, teachers can access real and authentic (for the most part) materials for their reading lessons. This means that even prescribed "boring" textbooks can be supplemented with more authentic materials that can include such items as restaurant menus, holiday/travel catalogs, and newspapers, to name a few.

2. Make reading the major activity of the reading lesson.

Some teachers have a habit of standing in front of their classes and spending the majority of class time just talking about reading, while their students do not get any time to practice reading. Reading classes should have a sustained period of actual reading, during which writing, speaking, and listening are not emphasized. Obviously, integrated lessons will take place when the teacher must orally present prereading activities, and students may be given postreading activities that include writing, speaking, and listening.

3. Have a specific objective for each lesson.

Each reading lesson should have some specific objective that can be achieved during that lesson. This could be as simple as getting the students to use prediction in its various forms: Predict the story from the heading, predict the paragraph from the topic sentence, predict the ending of the story after reading the introduction, and so on. The Appendix at the end of this chapter (from Farrell, 2006) is an example of a lesson that has a specific focus and a specific objective as follows:

- *Language focus:* Reading.
- *Topic:* Sport.
- *Objectives:* To teach the students to skim to find the main idea of the passage.
- *Prior knowledge:* Students have learned how to locate information by reading and finding the main sentence of each paragraph. This

lesson is to practice increasing their reading speed by scanning and skimming for information.

- *Materials and equipment:* Article from book on sport; overhead projector / overhead transparency; whiteboard.

All five aspects of lesson preparation are interrelated, and one cannot function without the other. For example, knowledge of the students' prior experiences will influence what specific objective(s) the teacher will focus on, and this in turn will influence the materials that the teacher chooses to achieve the objective.

4. Use activities that allow students to bring their own experiences to their reading.

One activity that will encourage our students to have a personal connection to a reading lesson is to get them to attempt predictions using the KWL strategy (Ogle, 1989). This acronym stands for three questions that students can ask when they have been given a reading assignment:

1. What do I **K**now?

2. What do I **W**ant to know?

3. What have I **L**earned?

These questions ask about the students' prior knowledge of a topic and motivate them to seek answers for their own questions, not the usual ten questions asked in most school texts. These questions can be answered by having the students write quickly all they know about the topic (What do I know?). Students can then skim their textbooks and compose a list of questions that tell what they would like to learn about the topic (What do I want to know?). Students are actually focusing on specific aspects of the topic while they are reading. Finally, students can be debriefed about what they have learned as a result of reading the topic or text. This can be performed orally or in writing. The KWL method also encourages integrated lessons.

5. Focus your instruction on teaching, not testing.

This principle has already been covered in earlier chapters, but it is no harm to mention it again, because the whole idea of teaching reading is to instruct our students to be able to comprehend unfamiliar texts. Thus the mantra of this book is: "I am a teacher, not a tester." How often do we see our students plunging into a text in order to answer comprehension questions and then become frustrated at their inability to find the answers to the correct questions? A testing focus will not generate independent, strategic readers. Testing or assessment has a place *after* students have been taught effective methods of comprehending the text.

6. Divide lessons into pre-, during- and postreading phases.

Teachers can introduce the lesson objective to the students at the beginning of the lesson and also encourage the students to activate their prior knowledge on the topic. This can be achieved by having students skim or scan the passage in order to generally orient them into the lesson. Next, the lesson should focus on the instructional objective—teaching a strategy or practicing a strategy already taught—and this should take up the majority of the class time. After the students have read and focused on the main part of the lesson, some closure is necessary to ease them out of the lesson. At this stage of the reading lesson, teachers can evaluate whether the lesson has been effective or whether it needs further reinforcement (in the form of assigned homework).

7. Choose appropriate reading materials.

It is important for teachers of reading to ELLs to take some time also to reflect on the materials or texts their students are asked to read. This is because materials can be used to support and enhance techniques and strategies that teachers focus on within a reading lesson. Of course, in many cases the textbook may have already been chosen by the school (as in a set curriculum). However, teachers can certainly adapt these materials to their own particular needs. They can also choose supplementary reading materials, depending on the needs of their students and the purpose of the reading class. The following criteria (in the form of questions) may be helpful for reading teachers when choosing a textbook:

- What are the goals of the reading course, and will this textbook help accomplish these goals?
- What is the reading proficiency level of the students in general?
- What approach to or theory of reading does the textbook reflect? Is it top-down, bottom-up, both, or something else?
- What is the content of the book? Is it authentic and appropriate for the students' needs and the curriculum needs?
- What kinds of exercises are included in each chapter? Do they include pre-, during-, and postreading exercises in each chapter?
- Is the vocabulary appropriate and relevant considering the proficiency levels of the students? Do the vocabulary exercises have the students practice techniques other than memorization, for example,

guessing the meanings of words (in context) they have never seen before?

- Is the general format and layout clear and easy to follow?

When choosing a specific reading passage for ELLs Day and Bamford (1998) suggest that the most important decision teachers consider is the level of interest their students have in the topic of the passage. In fact, according to Nutall (1996, p. 29) the single most important factor for the success of a reading class for ELLs is choosing passages that are interesting, and she says that this is "more critical than either the linguistic level of the text or its exploitability." Nutall (1996, p. 30) thus recommends that the teacher of reading to ELLs should attempt to discover if the passage will

- tell the student things they don't already know,
- introduce them to new and relevant ideas or make them think about things they haven't thought about before,
- help them understand the way people feel or think (e.g., people with different backgrounds, problems, or attitudes from their own), and/or
- make them want to read for themselves (to continue a story, find out more about a subject, and so on).

Teachers can calculate the readability of a text as well as the grade level by simply using Microsoft Word software. The procedure of checking includes the following steps:

1. Type the text into a file in Microsoft Word.

2. From the dropdown menu under Tools, select Options.

3. Select the Spelling & Grammar tab in the window that pops up, and make sure the box by "Show readability statistics" is marked. This box cannot be checked unless grammar is checked with spelling.

4. Close the window, return to the document, and run the spell-checker, which will check the grammar too.

5. When the spelling and grammar check is finished, readability statistics will be displayed.

In addition, the following questions can be asked by teachers when choosing particular materials for a reading lesson for ELLs:

- What types of language do the materials produce?
- Do materials provide effective models of language?

- Are the materials pitched at the correct/appropriate level of proficiency?
- Are the materials interesting?
- Are they visually appealing?
- What is the role of the materials in the lesson?
- Can the materials be adapted to better meet students' needs? How—by adding to, deleting from, or reorganizing them? Why?
- Do the materials match the pedagogical objectives of the lesson? That is, do they align with a specific teaching focus?
- Do they match the learning styles of the students?
- Are the paper reading materials and technological resources (CD-ROMs, videos) matched well?

REFLECTION

- What is your understanding of the principles outlined above?
- Can you add more principles?
- What are the factors you consider when choosing a particular passage for your students to read?

FROM READING LESSON TO READING CURRICULUM

So far we have mostly focused on individual teachers' reading lessons for ELLs, but we should also be aware that each lesson and individual teacher's course syllabus is a part of an overall reading curriculum set by a department, school, or school district. Usually, reading curriculum consists of a list of reading abilities that have to be developed, and as a result, tested (Aebersold & Field, 1997). Aebersold and Field (1997, p. 193) maintain that a basic reading curriculum will include the following:

- A clear statement of the mission of the reading program as a whole.
- A statement of the program's philosophy of how students develop their ability to read in the second/subsequent language.
- A statement as to how teachers should teach reading.
- An analysis of the students and their needs.
- A schedule for the reading program and an assessment of student progress within the program.
- A statement of the goals of each course within the program.
- A statement on assessment of student progress within the course.

Teachers of reading to ELLs will no doubt be able to interpret and adapt the reading program's curriculum to their own particular needs, because as Aebersold and Field (1997, p. 193) correctly point out, "Learners do not come in standardized forms, nor do teachers." It is a pity though, as many teachers of reading to ELLs already know that curriculum planners rarely, if ever, consult teachers when they plan and develop a reading curriculum. However, as we are also very well aware, it is the teacher who must implement such a curriculum and will usually do so in his or her own way.

CONCLUSION

This chapter has suggested that teachers of reading to ELLs should develop focused lesson plans that have their students practice effective reading strategies that enable them to read successfully. Effective lesson planning will not only help orient reading teachers but also help orient students throughout each reading lesson. In addition, we teachers should be aware that ELLs may come from first language backgrounds and cultures that have different ideas about how reading lessons should take place. Consequently, we should become familiar with our ELLs' cultural backgrounds and preferred learning styles so that we can accommodate (rather than suppress) these styles in our reading lessons.

Appendix to Chapter 7

LESSON PLAN

Time: 12 p.m. to 12:35 p.m.

Subject: English Language

Class: English

Language Focus: Reading

Topic: Sport

Objectives: To teach the students to skim to find the main idea of the passage

Prior Knowledge: Students have learned how to locate information by reading and finding the main sentence of each paragraph. This lesson is to practice increasing their reading speed by scanning and skimming for information.

Materials:
1. Reading materials—article from book on sport.
2. Overhead projector/overhead transparencies.
3. Whiteboard.

(Continued)

Step	Time	Tasks (Teacher, T)	Tasks (Student S)	Interaction	Purpose
1	5–10 min.	**Opening:** Introduction to the topic, sport. T activates schema for sport. T asks students to help him/her write down different kinds of sports on the whiteboard for 3 min.	**Listen** Ss shout out the answer to the question as T writes the answers on the board.	T ◄—► Ss	Arouse interest.
		T asks students to rank their favorite sports in order of importance.	T writes the answers.	T ◄—► Ss	Activate schema for sport.
2	5–7 min.	Teacher distributes handout on sports schedule from the newspaper.	Ss read the handout and answer the questions.	Ss ◄—► T	Focus attention of Ss on the concept of skimming for general gist with authentic materials.
		T asks Ss to read it quickly and answer the true/false questions that follow it within 3 min.	Ss call out their answers to T.	T ◄—► Ss	
		T goes over the answers.	Ss check their answers.	Ss ◄—► T	
3	15 min.	T tells students that they just practiced skimming to get the general meaning or gist of a passage.	Ss read the handout and answer the questions.	(S ◄—► S possible)	Getting Ss to read passage quickly to get the overall meaning.
		T gives another handout on sport from the textbook (*New Clue*). T asks Ss to read and answer the true/false questions written on the paper within 5–7 min.	Ss call out their answers to T.	T ◄—► Ss	
		T asks Ss for answers and writes them on the board.	Ss check their answers.	T ◄—► Ss	
4	5 min.	T summarizes the importance of reading a passage quickly first in order to get the gist.			To remind students what they have just done and why—to develop pupil metacognitive awareness.
		T gives homework of reading the next day's newspaper front page story and writing down in four sentences the gist of the story.			
Follow-up:		Next lesson: T teaches Ss to skim to find the main idea of the passage.			

SOURCE: Farrell, 2006.

8 Promoting Extensive Reading for ELLs

So far we have been talking about what teachers can do to help teach reading explicitly and intensively so that we can help our students read systematically as code breakers ("How do I crack this?"), text participants ("What does this mean?"), text users ("What do I do within this, here and now?"), and text analyzers ("What does all this do to me?") (Freebody & Luke, 1990, p. 15). In the previous chapter we also considered how to plan effective lessons for such intensive and explicit teaching of reading to ELLs. Now we need to consider how we can encourage our ELLs to read on their own and for fun in the same way they may play video games for fun.

This chapter covers reading for fun for ELLs, which is sometimes called *uninterrupted sustained silent reading* (USSR), *drop everything and read* (DEAR), or as it is used in this chapter, *extensive reading*. This type of reading calls for minimal intervention from the teacher, and according to Carrell and Carson (1997, pp. 49–50), it "generally involves rapid reading of large quantities of material . . . for general understanding, with the focus generally on meaning of what is being read than on language." The chapter outlines and discusses how teachers of reading to ELLs can promote extensive reading to their students so that they will eventually read more texts on their own both for information and for pleasure.

REFLECTION

- How can teachers encourage ELLs to read for fun by themselves?
- What kinds of materials do you think teachers should bring into their reading class to encourage their students to read for fun?

EXTENSIVE READING

Extensive reading is based on the theory that people learn to read by reading material outside the normal curriculum. Elley (1991, p. 375) shows how extensive reading can improve overall reading performance for beginning ELLs and suggests that "when immersed in meaningful text children appear to learn the language incidentally, and to develop a positive attitude toward books." The main point here is that ELLs begin to see reading as a fun activity and not the usual slog they may encounter when reading various texts in class. In addition, extensive reading also supports other aspects of an English language program; for example, it

- enhances language learning in such areas as spelling, vocabulary, grammar, and text structure;
- improves reading and writing skills;
- provides greater enjoyment of reading;
- develops a more positive attitude toward reading; and
- suggests a higher possibility of developing a reading habit. (adapted from Renandya & Jacobs, 2002, p. 298)

PROMOTING EXTENSIVE READING

Davis (1995, p. 329) has noted that an extensive reading program "is a supplementary class library scheme, attached to an English course in which pupils are given time, encouragement, and materials to read pleasurably, at their own level, as many books as they can, without the pressures of testing or marks." Day and Bamford (2002) list several principles that can be used when designing an extensive reading program especially for ELLs, some of which are the following:

1. The reading material is easy.

2. Students choose what they want to read from a variety of reading material.

3. Reading speed is usually faster rather than slower.

4. Reading is individual and silent.

5. The teacher is a role model.

6. Students should do something after reading.

1. The reading material is easy.

The first principle states that the reading material should be easy, and of course, this is relative to each student. However, the material should not be too basic, as the student may lose interest quickly. Research has indicated that when extensive reading is used to build fluency, then nearly all the words of the text the students are reading should be known to them. However, when the purpose of extensive reading is for language growth, then about 95 percent of the words in the text they are reading should be known. So, for extensive reading it is better that our students, especially those who lack confidence in reading, read easy texts (and lots of them) rather than more difficult ones. As Day and Bamford (2002, p. 1) maintain, "For extensive reading to be possible and for it to have the desired results, texts must be well within the learners' reading competence in the foreign language."

When choosing reading material, teachers can incorporate guided-reading instruction, where developmentally appropriate books (called *leveled books*) are read in small groups. Educators Irene C. Fountas and Gay Su Pinnell have devoted a whole Web site to leveled books, in which they sort over 18,000 books by level, genre, series, and publisher. (See www.FountasandPinnellLeveledBooks.com for more detailed information.)

2. Students choose what they want to read from a variety of reading material.

The second principle revolves around personal responsibility, as the student chooses his or her own reading material from a wide variety of topics and genres provided by the teacher. Then the student reads as much as possible with the idea that it is pleasurable and even informational. The teacher should include both fiction and nonfiction materials; however, when the purpose is pleasure reading, then it is always best to let the students self-select books based on their own reading interests. As Day and Bamford (2002, p. 1) again maintain, "Varied reading material not only encourages reading, it also encourages a flexible approach to reading. Learners are led to read for different reasons (e.g., entertainment; information; passing the time) and, consequently, in different ways (e.g., skimming; scanning; more careful reading)."

3. Reading speed is usually faster rather than slower.

The reading teacher should consider putting a time limit on the reading; otherwise some readers may read too slowly. However, this is not as straightforward as it may seem, because we do not want to push beginning readers too much and thus defeat the main purpose for extensive reading: reading for pleasure.

4. Reading is individual and silent.

What each student reads individually and silently has been called sustained silent reading (SSR) practice. During the class students are encouraged to read silently at their own pace. However, during this SSR time, teachers can help select a book, answer questions from learners, and observe learners' reactions toward reading. Nevertheless, individual teacher–student conversations should not disturb the other students who are reading.

5. The teacher is a role model.

While the students are reading extensively in class, the reading teacher should also read in the class. When students see that the teacher is reading, they may become curious about the book he or she is reading and may thus ask questions about the material. Reading teachers can then answer their students' questions, explain what they are reading and why they like this type of book, and explain that their reading interests may be different from their students' interests. Nutall (1996, p. 229) reminds teachers of reading to ELLs that "reading is caught, not taught." In leading by example, our attitude as readers ourselves is more important than our knowledge of the reading process; it will be among the most important factors that influence our students' desire to read extensively on their own.

6. Students should do something after reading.

One lingering doubt that teachers of reading to ELLs have after starting an extensive reading program is how they can be sure that their students have actually read the material they say they have. If extensive reading is to be for pleasure, then we must beware that we might spoil the enjoyment by asking our students comprehension questions and requiring them to write mindless summaries of the books they have read. How would you like to have to write a summary of the latest fiction book you have read?

Of course, if all the students are reading the same class book, then the teacher could also read it, and this makes checking the impact of that book easier. As Henry (1995, p. 52) has noted, "By reading what my students read, I become part of the community that forms within the class." But different groups can read different books and engage in different class activities that can be compared. Each student should keep a reading log of some sort about the material he or she is reading. This will enable students to draw on that information when discussing aspects of the books they have read. Then each class member can be asked to work individually or in pairs or groups to complete any of the following activities:

- Write a reaction letter to the author of the book, ask questions about it, and give comments—what you liked and did not like.
- Make a movie. "The Movie Version" (Farrell, 2004) is an activity where students cast actors for a movie based on a book they have read. "The Movie Version" is one alternative to the "boring book report."
- Students can also make a poster for the "movie of the book" or design and make a new book cover.
- Rather than a movie, students could also consider making a radio play from the story.

REFLECTION

- Do you think teachers should choose the reading materials for their students to read extensively? If your answer is yes, why? If it is no, why not?
- If you think teachers should choose reading materials for their students to read extensively, list some of these materials and say why these would be suitable.
- If you think students should be able to choose their own reading materials, what would you say if your students wanted to read an X-rated magazine or comic books, because they said they were interested in these materials?
- Do you think ELL reading teachers should have assignments attached to extensive reading activities? If they should, why? If not, why not?
- What type of reading assignments (if any) do you think are most appropriate and why?

CONCLUSION

Reading extensively helps ELLs move from a position of learning to read to reading to learn beyond their textbooks by encouraging them to read extensively on their own so that they can develop themselves both personally and professionally. As Renandya and Jacobs (2002, p. 300) maintain, "By encouraging our students to read extensively and showing them how to do so, we help them strengthen their grip on the efficacious tool of reading."

9 Authentic Reading Assessment for ELLs

Teachers cannot escape assessment, as it is essential to evaluate how effective our teaching methods are and to guide us in planning future reading lessons for our ELLs. This chapter first compares traditional and alternative modes of assessment and then discusses some of the classroom implications of the different types as well as the different roles of teachers and students for each. It suggests that alternative methods of assessment that are more authentic for ELLs can be used to compliment, rather than replace, traditional methods of assessment. This combination can give a clearer indication of how an ELL reading student is progressing and developing in a course.

TESTS

When we think of tests, we teachers usually visualize students sitting down with pencil or pen and writing on a piece of paper at a particular time in a particular place. They could be answering questions on a midterm exam, a final exam, a quiz, or an end-of-chapter test. With these, a teacher is trying to find out what the students have learned as a result of taking a specific course. These are called traditional paper-and-pencil tests, and more often than not, they focus on students' memorization abilities rather than on what the students can do with the information. At the end of a course, usually a teacher of reading to ELLs will look at the course goals of his or her reading class and try to measure (test) whether students have met these goals. Thus, Aebersold and Field (1997, p. 50) maintain that teachers of reading to ELLs must make "evaluative outcome statements" for particular goals. For example, they say a course goal could be (slightly adapted from Aebersold & Field, 1997, p. 50)

- "to be able to read information texts within the ELL's proficiency range and comprehend the topic and most of the ideas presented in this article."

The evaluative statement would then read,

- "Students will be able to read an informational text on a topic of general interest within their second/subsequent language proficiency range under timed conditions and correctly identify the topic and 80 percent of its main ideas with 75 percent accuracy."

Teachers of reading to ELLs must consider the types of evaluative tasks, such as that in the example above, that will determine students' final course grades. Usually teachers test their students to make these determinations. However, tests can be combined with more authentic reading assessments.

ASSESSMENT

The word *assessment* is more encompassing than the word *test*. It implies more of an ongoing process that includes tests but that covers more kinds of measurement than are possible with paper-and-pencil tests. As Aebersold and Field (1997, p. 167) point out, to assess ELLs "is to engage in an ongoing process that may include exams (periodic exams, midterms, finals), progress tests, quizzes, exercises worked in class or at home, or any other kind of testing or learning instrument." However, they maintain that to test "is to administer a single instrument that tests one or more aspects of a student's learning" (Aebersold & Field, 1997, p. 167). In other words, to assess a student does not always mean to test the student.

Thus, *assessment*, as the word is used in this chapter, includes traditional paper-and-pencil tests but also such items as affective assessment, portfolio assessment, and alternative assessment methods for reading instruction for

ELLs. Cohen and Cowen (2007) maintain that alternative assessment is more cognitively demanding than traditional methods of assessment, and as ELLs begin to interact more with peers and teachers, they discover that they become more collaborative while at the same time developing other language related skills as they negotiate meaning in a supportive environment.

Another way of talking about assessment is in terms of its purpose. The terms *formative* assessment and *summative* assessment have become quite common. McMillan (2008) suggests that *formative* assessment, or assessment of learning, occurs on a regular basis, can be used to document learning, and is designed to extend and encourage learning. Moreover, the term *formative* implies that the results of the assessment will inform the teacher of what students are learning and whether instruction needs to be adjusted while the course is being delivered. *Summative* assessment is used to determine how much students have learned, in other words, did the students learn what they were supposed to learn from taking a course. McMillan (2008) maintains that with summative assessment, there is little emphasis on using the results to improve learning or instruction. Formative assessment can be incorporated in the middle of a class, between classes or lessons, or in the middle of a course; summative assessment usually takes place at the end of the course.

Traditional Assessment

Traditional methods of assessing students remain very much in place in the education system, so teachers must be aware of what these are and what the advantages and disadvantages of each method are. For example, one of the most common tests of reading is the test of oral reading fluency; it is common because it is simple and quick. The basic idea of these tests is that oral reading fluency is a good measure of both the accuracy and speed with which a student can read, as measured in words read aloud correctly per minute. Either accuracy or speed by itself means nothing. ELLs who make no mistakes but read too slowly probably do not understand what they are reading as well as ELLs who read very quickly but guess and misidentify many words along the way.

To complete this test, teachers ask a student to read aloud an appropriate passage about 250 words in length. For the passage, teachers can use classroom materials that have been graded by a publisher, or a standardized measure of oral reading fluency, or they can ascertain the text's grade level using Chall and Dale's (1995) readability formula. I have problems with this method that are connected with my concerns about reading aloud in class, as was discussed in Chapter 1, Teaching Reading to ELLs.

Three other examples of the more popular traditional types of tests of reading comprehension include multiple-choice tests, short-answer tests, and essay tests.

Multiple-choice tests offer the test-takers a number of choices, one of which is the correct answer. Aebersold and Field (1997) maintain that this is the most familiar type of test used to check ELLs' reading comprehension. For example, this method is used in language assessment tests such as the Test of English as a Foreign Language (TOEFL) and multiple-choice questions appear in many ESL reading books.

In this type of test, there is one correct answer and all the other "distracters" are options that are incorrect. Two advantages of using multiple-choice tests are that they are easy to score either by hand or by machine and that the scoring is reliable. However, one major disadvantage is that these tests could promote guessing, and this can have an effect on the score. Multiple-choice tests check only recognition knowledge; you cannot be sure students actually understand the question, because they do not have to generate an answer.

In *short-answer tests*, students respond to a question by supplying a sentence or filling in a missing word in a statement. One advantage of these over multiple-choice tests is that students must generate an answer themselves, as opposed to recognizing the correct answer from a list. However, these tests are more difficult to score because of the longer response required, and this reduces the reliability of the test.

Essay tests are used when teachers want students to generate long answers in the form of a paragraph or a complete essay (usually consisting of five paragraphs). One advantage of an essay test is that it requires students to organize and synthesize their thoughts on a particular subject (depending on the essay question). As they compose their essays, students must also evaluate what information to include and not to include. However, herein lies a disadvantage; writing an essay in itself is difficult. Essays are also difficult to score because of the subjective nature of what a good essay is.

In the traditional mode of testing reading, there are also other tests, such as vocabulary tests in which ELLs are given word-matching exercises or lists of words they must define, but as Aebersold and Field (1997, p. 174) maintain, these vocabulary tests may mislead ELLs into thinking that "learning words is the only key to good reading." Another popular test of reading is the cloze test, where students are asked to insert the appropriate word where a word has been deleted from a passage. Usually the test designer deletes every nth word, so there is no variation to make the test valid. Again, Aebersold and Field (1997, p. 168) point out that the cloze test for ELLs may not be a valid or dependable test of reading comprehension, because ELLs "need to be taught appropriate test-taking strategies in order to perform well."

Alternative Assessment

Alternative assessment, in contrast to the traditional tests above, assumes that learning is not linear (from cognitive psychology findings) and that learning is ongoing. Cohen and Cowen (2007) suggest that assessment in general plays an important role in all aspects of education for ELLs, especially when placing ELLs into appropriate levels of instruction. For teachers of ELLs, assessment provides the necessary feedback that they can base future teaching decisions on. Another facet of alternative assessment is that students will attempt to connect this learning to their prior knowledge in an attempt to make an understanding.

Alternative assessment offers many advantages to teachers and ELLs. An emphasis on meaning, rather than form, underlies many of the new assessment instruments. Many alternative assessment methods, such as think-aloud protocols, seek to investigate process. Furthermore, and linked to other chapters in this book, an understanding of the social nature of learning has led to the inclusion of peer assessment and to the use of group tasks in assessment.

Some disadvantages of alternative assessment instruments are that they are often more time-consuming and costly than traditional instruments as well as less reliable in terms of consistency of scoring. Nevertheless, they are gaining prominence due to dissatisfaction with traditional modes of assessment, which are faulted for not capturing vital information about students' competence in their second language.

We do not have to do away with the traditional tests altogether, as they can be transformed to be more like alternative assessments as follows:

- True-false tests can use higher-order questions by including scenarios, essays, or situations. Students must then choose which following statement represents a likely analysis or trend, and they can be asked to make predictions about a passage or idea presented in the passage.
- Multiple-choice tests can be similarly changed, and the questions can get students to make conclusions or generalizations about a case study or situation. Taking it one step further, ELLs can be asked to justify their choices and why they rejected certain answers.
- Essay questions can be changed away from requiring students to provide facts to getting them to do something with the facts. ELLs can be asked to analyze situations in an essay and to give reasons to support their views.

AUTHENTIC ASSESSMENT

As Aebersold and Field (1997, p. 168) have suggested, alternative reading assessment for ELLs is a shift away from using assessment as a way to "keep students in their place." Instead, they say, alternative assessment helps students understand where they are situated in their development. Cohen and Cowen (2007) note that it may be difficult to assess ELLs because of the different languages they operate in with different levels of proficiency. For example, an ELL may be a very proficient reader in his or her first language but may not be as proficient a reader in the second/subsequent language, English. Therefore, Cohen and Cowen (2007) and others support more authentic performance-based assessments for ELLs, as these can provide more specific feedback to students to support their learning.

Principles of Authentic Reading Assessment for ELLs

The following guidelines may be useful for teachers of reading to ELLs when considering assessment for their students (adapted from Aebersold & Field, 1997):

1. Keep the course objectives clearly in mind.

Teachers usually assess their students because they want to give their students a chance to demonstrate what they have learned as a result of taking a course. So, when teachers are writing a test for this purpose, they should always keep track of the course objectives and not test material that has not been covered. Aebersold and Field (1997) suggest, for example, that in an extensive reading course, it would not be useful to ask ELLs to write a final exam that requires them to recall specific details of the text, because memorizing such details is not the objective of extensive reading classes.

2. Carefully match the test to what is to be tested.

Connected to the first principle (above), the test itself should be similar to the curriculum of the course. This concerns the validity of a test. For example, if a teacher just completed a unit of reading that was devoted to activating ELLs' prior knowledge, then one would expect a test that covered activation of prior knowledge only and not recall of the meaning of specific words in that unit. Thus, content and construct validity of the test would not be a concern.

3. Recognize the potential for bias and variation.

Teachers should realize that their ELLs come from many different cultural backgrounds and that some types of tests may be biased in favor of certain cultural groups, while the same tests may disadvantage other groups. Thus, Aebersold and Field (1997, p. 177) maintain that it is the teacher's "responsibility to investigate students' attitudes and beliefs about reading." Also, certain tests (the entire test or parts of the test) may be offensive to a certain subgroup of students. One way teachers can reduce this possible bias or variation is to use nontraditional or alternative means of assessment (as outlined in this chapter).

Authentic Reading Assessment for ELLs

Rather than using the more traditional approaches outlined earlier in the chapter, teachers of reading to ELLs may thus want to consider using the following authentic reading assessment methods:

- Portfolios
- Peer assessment
- Self-reports
- Anecdotal records
- Attitude scales
- Informal reading inventory

Portfolios

A portfolio is a systematic collection of information about a student that consists of evidence of that student's accomplishments and skills. ELLs are responsible for compiling their own portfolios, and the portfolios must be updated as the students develop and add to their achievements. Most important, portfolios encourage ELLs to take more responsibility and ownership for their own learning.

The contents of student portfolios vary, but usually they include samples of a student's work related to his or her reading. Contents can include the student's list of extensive reading books, magazines, or other such materials; assignments the student completed during extensive reading time; and other reading assignments completed during the semester. Although the contents of students' portfolios may vary greatly, teachers can design guidance sheets to suggest a familiar structure for each portfolio entry as follows:

Description: What is this entry?

Reason: Why did I include this entry?

Opinion: Why do I think this entry is important? Why am I proud about this entry?

Reflection: What did I accomplish with this entry?

Teacher comments (optional): Teachers can add comments after each entry.

Drawbacks of portfolios are that they take time to compile, they take time to review and evaluate, and it is difficult to devise a scoring system for such an assessment. Teachers must devise scoring guides that are neither too detailed, so that evaluators are overwhelmed, nor so general as to render the scoring process too subjective. The key is to come up with a balanced scoring system.

Peer Assessment

Another alternative and authentic reading assessment is the involvement of peers in the assessment process. ELLs evaluate each other on aspects of reading that include levels of reading participation, work samples, and behavior in class. Because ELLs know they are also going to be evaluated by their peers, they tend to become more cooperative when they are working with other peers. Therefore, it is important that each student knows what criteria will be used for this evaluation.

Students can rate their peers in many ways. For example, if teachers want to retain some control, they can allow the students to use the same rating instruments that the teacher uses when students give a presentation in class. Peers can fill in the rating scale designed by the teacher (either along with the teacher or instead of the teacher). Alternatively, the students themselves can design their own rating instruments with the guidance of their teacher. For example, they can rate their peers in terms of items that the teacher may not be most competent to know because he or she does not interact with the students outside class. This grade can add a new dimension to assessment and even make it look like a more equitable measuring instrument in the students' eyes:

Which student(s) read the most in class?

Which student(s) read the least in class?

Which student(s) share reading materials with their fellow students the most?

Which student(s) share reading materials with their fellow students the least?

Which student(s) do their reading homework the best?

Which student(s) never do their reading homework?

Which student(s) do well on all reading assessments and reading tests?

Which student(s) do not do well on reading assessments and reading tests but work hard?

Which student(s) are best at reading?

Table 9.1 shows a form that teachers can use to provide structure for a peer assessment activity. For this activity, the teacher arranges the students in groups of three, and each has a chance to assess the other two. One student first acts as observer and checks each time he or she observes the other two students read, write, or do whatever is being assessed. (Teachers will want to change the items being observed depending on their needs and the needs of their students.)

Table 9.1   Peer-to-peer in-class assessment

Name of Student	*Reading?*	*Writing?*	*Active in group?*	*Asks questions?*	*Helps others?*
Student 1					
Student 2					

Name of Student Observer (Student 3):   Date:

In this way teachers can obtain extra information about their students—information about the students from the students. The teacher must be careful to realize however, that some of the students' observations of their peers' performances may have an element of assessment of their peers' social acceptance in a group or class, rather than being simply an honest answer about the students' academic abilities. Therefore, teachers should make sure they carefully explain the reason for using this rating system to their students before they use it.

Self-Reports

Self-reports are a useful way of obtaining information from ELLs. These can be conducted in a face-to-face *interview* format, or students may decide that they want to record their own *self-reports on tape* (audio or video) for teachers to listen to or watch later. The interview should be a discussion rather than a police-style interrogation of the student.

Alternatively, teachers or students can draw up a self-report questionnaire or *inventory* that the students can fill out when they have time, as this is less time-consuming that the interview process.

Anecdotal Records

Teachers know their students better than anybody else. They know whole students in terms of their likes and dislikes, their abilities, their willingness to talk in class, how they take tests, and how they generally prefer to learn. This knowledge is built up from the teachers' daily observations of their students in action in their classrooms (and outside the classrooms). For example, a teacher may know that one student, Sarah, is a really good researcher but does not like and does not do well in written tests about what she has read.

Instead of relying solely on test results, teachers can take this kind of information into consideration when assigning grades to students. Teachers can do this by collecting anecdotal records. These are factual descriptions of events or incidents that involve specific students in terms of their learning. Teachers should write these down as soon as they happen rather than rely on selective memory. One notebook could be assigned for each student the teacher has under his/her supervision, or the teacher can use index cards for each entry for each student and then file all the cards for each student under that student's name. These are also very useful for teachers when preparing for parent-teacher conferences.

Attitude Scales

These scales, usually designed by the teacher, can be a useful means of gauging students' feelings and opinions about various aspects of their schooling such as *classroom activities, peers, school events, teachers, and administrators*. These scales can give teachers a more detailed understanding of their students' preferences for certain reading activities and the like and can aid teachers with their planning, both inside and outside the classroom.

For example, teachers can design an attitude scale that measures how much their students like such activities as predicting, previewing, scanning, skimming, writing summaries, extensive reading, and other such activities carried out in class. Teachers can obtain useful information from these scales about their students' perceptions of certain activities and can use this information for lesson planning and course revisions. However, teachers should also realize that sometimes ELLs may have a negative perception of an activity that they cannot do or understand, regardless of how educational, important, or useful the activity may be.

Because teachers are the people closest to their students, they are the best to judge the value of the overall responses.

Informal Reading Inventory

The informal reading inventory (IRI) is an informal assessment that diagnoses a student's reading strengths and weaknesses, "thereby [helping teachers to make] appropriate decisions regarding classroom instruction" (Cohen & Cowen, 2007, p. 376). In this activity, usually done at the beginning of the course, teachers have their ELLs read from graded word lists and passages and then have them answer comprehension questions that can suggest their reading levels. To assess a student's progress, these levels can be checked at different intervals as the course progresses. Cohen and Cowen (2007, p. 376) suggest that teachers can use this assessment to identify the following three levels of reading material for each ELL:

1. *Independent level:* This is the highest level of material that the ELL can read fluently and accurately while requiring little or no instructional assistance from the teacher.

2. *Instructional level:* This is material that the ELL can read with approximately 90 percent accuracy, requiring limited instructional assistance from the teacher. This is the most important level for a teacher to determine, because this is the level at which instruction in the classroom should be targeted.

3. *Frustration level:* This is material that the ELL cannot read fluently or with understanding, even with instructional support. At this level, the child displays evident frustration, showing stress, anxiety, and tension; reading is characterized by slow, word-by-word reading.

The IRI, according to Cohen and Cowen (2007), is very useful for teachers of reading to ELLs, because it can help teachers select appropriate level textbooks (if they are allowed to), design reading instruction for individual ELLs, and group students at appropriate levels for vocabulary, reading comprehension, and guided reading activities. Many teachers of reading to ELLs have reported this last item as being a constant frustration in classes that have ELLs at many different levels of language proficiency. With the IRI, teachers can at least ascertain an estimated reading level at which each ELL is functioning so that "appropriate learning opportunities can be designed and implemented" (Cohen & Cowen, 2007, p. 376) for each ELL.

Of course, teachers of reading to ELLs need not design assessment tasks alone. For example, when designing assessments that take real-life situations into consideration, teachers need to consider what people do in their everyday jobs. In order to do this, teachers can involve the ELLs by getting them to interview people in various careers. The interview should include questions about how important reading is in the career and what the most important type of reading is that the individual needs to succeed in work and life. In this way, students can begin to see relationships between the real world and what they learn in school.

ELLs can be further involved by having them set the criteria by which their assignments will be assessed. These criteria should be agreed upon before the start of the assignment so that each student (and the teacher) is aware of what is required.

CONCLUSION

This chapter has outlined both traditional assessment methods and alternative assessment methods that teachers of reading to ELLs can consider. The chapter suggests that alternative assessment instruments have been developed that complement (but do not necessarily replace) traditional instruments. Alternative authentic assessment instruments attempt to mirror real-life conditions more closely, where people struggle through process while arriving at product. Thus, assessment captures vital information about ELLs' linguistic development through the process of learning.

References

Aebersold, J. A., & Field, M. L. (1997). *From reader to reading teacher.* Cambridge, UK: Cambridge University Press.

Amer, A. A. (1997). The effect of the teacher's reading aloud on the reading comprehension of EFL students. *English Language Teaching Journal, 51*(1), 43–48.

Anderson, N. (2003). Reading. In D. Nunan (Ed.), *Practical English language teaching* (pp. 67–86). New York: McGraw-Hill.

Anthony, H. M., Pearson, P. D., & Raphael, T. E. (1993). Reading comprehension: A selected review. In L. M. Cleary & M. D. Linn (Eds.), *Linguistics for teachers* (pp. 250–298). New York: McGraw-Hill.

Au, K. (1980). Participation structures in a reading lesson with Hawaiian children: Analysis of a culturally appropriate instructional event. *Anthropology and Education Quarterly, 11,* 91–115.

August, D., & Shanahan, T. (2006). *Developing literacy in second-language learners: Report of the National Literacy Panel on Language-Minority Children and Youth.* Mahwah, NJ: Erlbaum.

Block, C. C., & Israel, S. (2005). *Reading first and beyond.* Thousand Oaks, CA: Corwin Press.

Block, C. C., Rodgers, L., & Johnson, R. (2004). *Comprehension process instruction.* New York: Guilford.

Carrell, P. L. (1985). Facilitating ESL reading by teaching text structure. *TESOL Quarterly, 19,* 727–752.

Carrell, P. L. (1992). Awareness of text structure: Effects on recall. *Language Learning, 42,* 1–20.

Carrell, P. L. (1998). Can reading strategies be taught? *Australian Review of Applied Linguistics, 21,* 1–20.

Carrell, P. L., & Carson, J. G. (1997). Extensive and intensive reading in an EAP setting. *ESP Journal, 16,* 47–60.

Chall, J., & Dale, E. (1995). *Readability revisited.* Cambridge, MA: Brookline.

Chamot, A. U., & El-Dinary, P. B. (1999). Children's learning strategies in immersion classrooms. *The Modern Language Journal, 83,* 319–341.

Clark, K., & Graves, M. (2005). Scaffolding students' comprehension of text. *The Reading Teacher, 58,* 570–580.

Cohen, V. L., & Cowen, J. E. (2007). *Literacy for children in an information age: Teaching reading, writing, and thinking.* Belmont, CA: Wadsworth.

Collins, A., Brown, J. S., & Holum, A. (1991). Cognitive apprenticeship: Making thinking visible. *American Educator, 6,* 38–46.

Coxhead, A. (2000). A new academic word list. *TESOL Quarterly, 34*(2), 213–238.

Davis, C. (1995). Extensive reading: An expensive extravagance? *English Language Teaching Journal, 49,* 329–336.

Day, R. R., & Bamford, J. (1998). *Extensive reading in the second language classroom.* Cambridge, UK: Cambridge University Press.

Day, R. R., & Bamford, J. (2002). Top ten principles for teaching extensive reading. *Reading in a Foreign Language, 14*(2) [Electronic version]. Retrieved May 20, 2006, from http://nflrc.hawaii.edu/rfl

Duke, N. K., & Pearson, P. D. (2002). Effective practices for developing reading comprehension. In A. E. Farstrup & J. Samuels (Eds.), *What research has to say about reading instruction* (3rd ed., pp. 203–242). Newark, DE: International Reading Association.

Elley, W. B. (1991). Acquiring literacy in a second language: The effect of book-based programs. *Language Learning, 41*, 375–411.

Eskey, D. E. (2002). Reading and the teaching of L2 reading. *TESOL Journal, 11*, 5–9.

Eskey, D. E., & Grabe, W. (1988). Interactive models for second language reading: Perspectives on instruction. In P. L. Carrell, J. Devine, & D. E. Eskey (Eds.), *Interactive approaches to second language reading* (pp. 223–238). New York: Cambridge University Press.

Farrell. T. S. C. (2000). Activating prior knowledge in L2 reading: The teacher's role. *Guidelines, 22*(1), 10–16.

Farrell, T. S. C. (2002). Lesson planning. In J. C. Richards & W. A. Renandya (Eds.), *Methodology in language teaching: An anthology of current practice* (pp. 30–39). New York: Cambridge University Press.

Farrell, T. S. C. (2004). The movie version. In J. Bamford & R. R. Day, *Extensive reading activities for teaching language* (pp. 143–144). New York: Cambridge University Press.

Farrell, T. S. C. (2005). Teaching reading strategies: "It really takes time!" In G. Poedjosoedarmo (Ed.), *Innovative approaches to reading & writing instruction* (pp. 71–81). RELC Anthology Series 46. Singapore: SEAMEO Regional Language Centre.

Farrell, T. S. C. (2006). *Succeeding with English language learners: A guide for beginning teachers*. Thousand Oaks, CA: Corwin Press.

Fisk, C., & Hurst, B. (2003). Paraphrasing for comprehension. *The Reading Teacher, 57*, 182–185.

Freebody, P., & Luke, A. (1990). 'Literacies' programmes: Debates and demands in cultural context. *Prospect, 11*, 7–16.

Glasgow, N., & Farrell, T. S. C. (2007). *What successful literacy teachers do*. Thousand Oaks, CA: Corwin Press.

Good, R. H., Simmons, D., & Kame'enui, E. (2001). The importance and decision-making utility of a continuum of fluency-based indicators of foundational reading skills for third-grade high-stakes outcomes. *Scientific Studies of Reading, 5*, 257–286.

Grabe, W. (1986). Theoretical foundations. In F. Dubin, D. E. Eskey, & W. Grabe (Eds.), *Teaching second language reading for academic purposes* (pp. 3–23). Reading, MA: Addison-Wesley.

Grabe, W., & Stoller, F. L. (2002). *Teaching and researching reading*. New York: Longman.

Graves, M. F. (1984). Selecting vocabulary to teach in the intermediate and secondary grades. In J. Flood (Ed.), *Promoting reading comprehension* (pp. 245–260). Newark, DE: International Reading Association.

Harris, T. L., & Hodges, R. E. (1995). *The literacy dictionary*. Newark, DE: International Reading Association.

Henry, J. (1995). *If not now: Developmental readers in the college classroom*. Portsmouth, NH: Boynton/Cook, Heinemann.

Hunt, A., & Beglar, D. (2002). Current research and practice in teaching vocabulary. In J. Richards & W. Renandya (Eds.), *Methodology and language teaching. An anthology of current practice* (pp. 258–266). New York: Cambridge University Press.

International Reading Association. (2006). *Position statements*. Retrieved May 19, 2007, from http://www.reading.org

Johnston, P. H. (1983). *Reading comprehension assessment: A cognitive basis*. Newark, DE: International Reading Association.

Kame'enui, E. J., & Simmons, D. C. (2001). Introduction to this special issue: The DNA of reading fluency. *Scientific Studies of Reading, 5*, 203–210.

Kaplan, R. B. (1987). Cultural thought patterns revisited. In U. Conner & R. B. Kaplan (Eds.), *Writing across languages* (pp. 9–21). Reading, MA: Addison-Wesley.

Koda, K. (2005). *Insights into second language reading*. New York: Cambridge University Press.

McEwan, E. K. (2002). *Teach them all to read*. Thousand Oaks, CA: Corwin Press.

McMillan, J. H. (2008). *Assessment essentials for standards-based education*. Thousand Oaks, CA: Corwin Press.

Mikulecky, B. (1990). *A short course in teaching reading skills.* New York: Addison-Wesley.

Nation, I. S. P. (2002). *Managing vocabulary learning.* RELC Portfolio Series 2. Singapore: SEAMEO Regional Language Centre.

Nation, I. S. P. (2003). Vocabulary. In D. Nunan (Ed.), *Practical English language teaching* (pp. 129–152). New York: McGraw-Hill.

Nation, P., & Coady, J. (1988). Vocabulary and reading. In R. Carter & M. McCarthy (Eds.), *Vocabulary and language teaching* (pp. 97–110). New York: Longman.

Nutall, C. (1996). *Teaching reading skills in a foreign language* (2nd ed.). Oxford, UK: Heinemann.

Ogle, D. (1989). KWL: A teaching model that develops active reading of expository text. *Reading Teacher, 39,* 546–570.

Palincsar, A. S. (1986). The role of dialogue in providing scaffolded instruction. *Educational Psychologist, 21,* 73–98.

Papalia, A. (1987). Interaction of reader and text. In W. M. Rivers (Ed.), *Interactive language teaching* (pp. 70–82). Cambridge, UK: Cambridge University Press.

Pardo, L. S. (2004). What every teacher needs to know about comprehension. *The Reading Teacher, 58,* 272–280.

Paris, S. G., Wasik, B. A., & Turner, J. C. (1991). The development of strategic readers. In R. Barr, M. L. Kamil, P. B. Mosenthal, & P. D. Pearson (Eds.), *Handbook of reading research* (Vol. II, pp. 609–640). New York: Longman.

Phillips, S. (1972). Participation structures and communicative competence: Warm Springs children in community and classroom. In C. B. Cazden (Ed.), *Functions of language in the classroom* (pp. 370–394). New York: Teachers College Press.

Rasinski, T. V. (2003). *The fluent reader: Oral reading strategies for building word recognition, fluency, and comprehension.* New York: Scholastic Professional Books.

Renandya, W., & Jacobs, G. (2002). Extensive reading: Why aren't we all doing it? In J. Richards & W. Renandya (Eds.), *Methodology and language teaching. An anthology of current practice* (pp. 295–302). New York: Cambridge University Press.

Richards, J. C. (1990). *The language teaching matrix.* Cambridge, UK: Cambridge University Press.

Richards, J. C. (1998). *Beyond methods.* Cambridge, UK: Cambridge University Press.

Rivera, K. (1999). From developing one's voice to making oneself heard: Affecting language policy from the bottom up. In T. Huebner & K. Davis (Eds.), *Socio-political perspectives on language policy and language planning in the USA* (pp. 333–346). Amsterdam: Benjamins.

Rumelhart, D. E. (1980). Schemata: The building blocks of cognition. In R. J. Spiro, B. C. Bruce, & W. F. Brewer (Eds.), *Theoretical issues in reading comprehension: Perspectives from psychology, linguistics, artificial intelligence and education* (pp. 33–58). Hillsdale, NJ: Erlbaum.

Shaywitz, B. A., Shaywitz, S. E., Blachman, B., Pugh, K. R., Fulbright, R., Skudlarski, P., et al. (2004). Development of left occipito-temporal systems for skilled reading following a phonologically-based intervention in children. *Biological Psychiatry, 55,* 926–933.

Smith, F. (1978). *Understanding reading: A psycholinguistic analysis of reading and learning to read.* New York: Holt, Rinehart and Winston.

Stanovich, K. E. (1980). Towards an interactive-compensatory model of individual differences in the development of reading fluency. *Reading Research Quarterly, 16,* 32–71.

Stauffer, R. G. (1969). *Directing reading maturity as a cognitive process.* New York: Harper & Row.

Tierney, R. J., & Pearson, P. D. (1994). Learning to learn from text: A framework for improving classroom practice. In R. B. Ruddell, M. R. Ruddell, & H. Singer (Eds.), *Theoretical models and processes of reading* (4th ed., pp. 496–513). Newark, DE: International Reading Association.

Winograd, P., & Hare, V. C. (1988). Direct instruction of reading comprehension strategies: The nature of teacher explanation. In C. E. Weinstein, E. T. Goetz, & P. A. Alexander (Eds.), *Learning and study strategies: Issues in assessment instruction and evaluation* (pp. 121–139). San Diego, CA: Academic Press.

Zygouris-Coe, V., Wiggins, M. B., & Smith, L. H. (2004). Engaging students with the text: The 3-2-1 strategy. *The Reading Teacher, 58*(4), 381–384.

Index